ANTON CORBIJN

Allegro war das zweite von mittlerweile 14
Photograph und Filmemacher Anton Cor
öffentlicht hat. Nach *Famouz*, seinem Ers
radikal neuen Blick auf die Großen der Pop- und Rockszene praktisch über Nacht weltberühmt gemacht hatte, markierte *Allegro* zwei Jahre später bereits eine vielversprechende Weiterentwicklung seines photographischen Spektrums: Neben Klassikern in Schwarzweiß – Bono, David Bowie, Miles Davis, Sting, Tom Waits und vielen anderen – enthielt der Band, den wir jetzt als zweisprachige, deutsch-englische Ausgabe neu auflegen, erstmals auch Portraits und experimentelle Arbeiten in Farbe.

Seitdem hat Anton Corbijn sein Portrait-Pantheon um die großen Namen aus der Welt der Musik und Kunst, der Literatur und des Films ständig erweitert. Heute zählt er nicht nur zu den wichtigsten Photographen seiner Generation, auch als Regisseur und Produzent mehrerer Kinofilme sorgte er international für Aufsehen, zuletzt mit der John Le Carré-Verfilmung *A Most Wanted Man* (2014) und dem James Dean-Drama *Life* (2015).

Allegro was the second of meanwhile 14 photo books Dutch photographer and filmmaker Anton Corbijn has published with Schirmer/Mosel. After Famouz, his 1989 debut that made him and his radically new view of the heroes of Pop and Rock literally world-famous overnight. *Allegro*, published only two years later, marked the promising progress of his photographic arange: along with classics in black and white—Bono, David Bowie, Miles Davis, Sting, Tom Waits, and many others— the volume, now available in a bilingual German/English reprint, for the first time featured portraits and experimental works in color as well.

Since then Anton Corbijn has continuously expanded his pantheon of portraiture by major players from the worlds of music and art, literature and cinema. Today, he not only ranks among the most important photographers of his generation. He also catches international attraction as a movie director and producer, most recently with his John Le Carré adaptation *A Most Wanted Man* (2014) and his James Dean drama *Life* (2015).

Anton Corbijn

Allegro

Text
von / by
Els Barents

SCHIRMER/MOSEL

For help in creating this little book, that is by lack of a better description 'an interesting mix of my work at the time', when it was originally published in 1991, I wish to express thanks to ELS BARENTS, BONO, SIOUXSIE, BUDGIE, NASSIM, *SPIN*, *THE FACE*, *LA STYLE*, *OOR*, KOJI TATSUNO, YVONNE SPORRE, STOYA ("immer da"), BRIAN DOWLING AND MIKE SPRY, plus everyone in the photographs as well as all at Schirmer/Mosel.

A. C.

Illustration on the cover:
The Creatures, Seville, 1989

The text by Els Barents was translated from the Dutch by Paul Vincent, into German by Magda Moses and Bram Opstelten.

Lithography: NovaConcept, Berlin
Printing and binding: Gorenjski Tisk, Kranj

ISBN 978-3-8296-0794-0
A Schirmer/Mosel Production

Els Barents

WIE EIN KÖNIG IM STRANDKORB

A KING IN A DECKCHAIR

1991

Die Veröffentlichung des Photobandes *Famouz* 1989 bedeutete für Anton Corbijn einen Wendepunkt in seiner Laufbahn als Portraitphotograph der internationalen Popmusik-Szene. Über den begrenzten Kreis von Insidern hinaus fanden seine Arbeiten jetzt auch bei einem viel größeren Publikum Anerkennung. Aber Corbijn distanzierte sich von dem „Jugendtraum", den er zur Profession gemacht hatte. *Famouz* rundete gewissermaßen die erste Etappe eines Karriereverlaufs ab, der sich in fünfzehnjähriger, harter Arbeit mehr oder weniger „natürlich" ergeben hatte. Mit wachsendem Selbstbewusstsein räumte er jetzt dem Experiment mehr Platz ein. Das begann mit einer Erweiterung seines technischen Repertoires: neben das Schwarzweiß, das schon zu seinem Markenzeichen geworden war, trat beispielsweise die Farbe, gleichberechtigt und eigenständig. Dann folgten formale Veränderungen; das Bemühen um einen höheren Grad der Abstraktion führte zur Auseinandersetzung mit anderen, neuen Sujets. Neben den Portraits entstanden jetzt auch Stillleben, und er begann mit anonymen Modellen zu arbeiten. Leiten ließ er sich bei all diesen Erkundungen von seiner Fähigkeit, in Bildern zu denken, von seiner Faszination am Licht und seiner teils intuitiven, teils rational begründeten Überzeugung, dass er Fortschritte nur dann erzielen könne, wenn er sich nicht auf eine einzige Arbeitsmethode beschränkte. Die Unabhängigkeit, die ihm der Erfolg bot, investierte er gleich wieder: diesmal in die Unruhe und Neugierde, die ihn zum Weitergehen anspornten. In dem Interview, das dieser Einführung vorausging, benutzte Corbijn das Wort Angst – die Angst, zu stagnieren, bevor man die eigenen Fähigkeiten voll erkundet hat.

Das Bedürfnis, Abstand von der eigenen Arbeit zu gewinnen, wirkte sich schließlich auch auf sein zweites Buch aus. *Allegro* kam, ein gutes Jahr später, unter deutlich veränderten Bedingungen zustande. Während *Famouz* nicht nur inhaltlich, sondern auch von der Gestaltung her Corbijns persönliche Handschrift trägt, überließ er jetzt die Typographie und sogar die Zusammenstellung des Bildmaterials anderen. Auch bestand er nicht mehr darauf, seine Photographien ohne Vorwort oder einführenden Text zu präsentieren.

The publication of *Famouz* in 1989 marked a turning-point in Anton Corbijn's career as a portrait photographer of pop singers and musicians. Although this first book brought him much wider public acclaim than the insider re-putation he had previously enjoyed, Corbijn himself moved away from the 'boy's dream' he had chosen as a career. *Famouz* represented the completion of a natural cycle in the career he had spent 15 years' hard work building up. With new-found confidence, he created scope for experiment and exercised still greater self-discipline. A first priority was the broadening of his technical range, for example by introducing colour alongside black-and-white.

Subsequently the pursuit of a higher degree of abstraction had a formal impact, and he began using different subject matter. Besides portraits there were now also still-lifes and studies of anonymous models. The underlying constants in these explorations were his ability to think in images, his fascination with light and the conviction – half intuitive, half rational – that success need not be tied to one particular method. The material comfort brought by his breakthrough enabled him to indulge the restless urge to move on. In a preliminary interview, Corbijn talked of anxiety at the prospect of coming to a standstill after exploring only part of his own potential.

This need to distance himself from his own work is also reflected in the way his second book, *Allegro,* came into being almost a year later. Although *Famouz* bears his personal stamp in both content and form, he has now entrusted both typography and the layout of his visual material to others and abandoned his previous dislike of introductions. *Allegro* is a book at a turning point, a still from a journey in progress. The continuity of old and new work is just discernible, but the two are no longer based on a clearly-defined common premise, despite appearances. However, without being either able or willing to make it clear where he is heading, for the moment Corbijn is content to indicate the pace he is moving at.

How can one explain why a vicar's son, who until the age of thirteen was convinced of his vocation as a missionary, should at seventeen be pushing his way to the front at pop concerts and subsequently decide to

Allegro ist ein Buch an einem Wendepunkt, eine Momentaufnahme von unterwegs. Das frühere und das neue Werk berühren einander gerade noch, ein beiden gemeinsames Grundkonzept fehlt jedoch, auch wenn hier der erste Eindruck täuschen mag. Ohne erklären zu können oder zu wollen, wohin der Weg führen wird, gibt Corbijn fürs erste nur das Tempo an: allegro – „lebhaft, schnell".

Wie reimt es sich zusammen, dass ein Pfarrerssohn, der bis zu seinem dreizehnten Lebensjahr Missionar werden wollte, sich mit siebzehn in das Getümmel von Popkonzerten stürzt, sich mit seinem Photoapparat bis an die Rampe vordrängelt und beschließt, Portraitphotograph zu werden? Der künstlerische und geschäftliche Erfolg, den Anton Corbijn heute erfährt, scheint den gewohnten Existenzmustern jedenfalls zu widersprechen. Er selbst charakterisiert sich als Außenseiter; aufgewachsen in einem eher amusischen Klima und ohne besondere Ausbildung, plagt ihn ständig der Gedanke, zu wenig zu wissen.

Die Wege, die Corbijn in seiner Jugend ging, erinnern an das Märchen vom kleinen Hans, der von zu Hause wegläuft und in die weite Welt zieht – hinter der Musik und dem fahrenden Volk her. Variationen dieses unverkennbar romantischen Themas waren bis weit in die fünfziger Jahre hinein verbreitet; ein damals in Holland sehr beliebtes Kinderbuch, *Alleine auf der Welt,* belegt das ebenso wie Fellinis *La Strada.* Jemandem, der den mühsamen Prozess des Erwachsenwerdens in den sechziger Jahren durchlebte, blieb diese Vorstellung allerdings fremd.

Trotzdem, gewisse Anzeichen von Abenteuerlust kann man Corbijns Werk nicht absprechen. Erst jetzt, nach der Veröffentlichung von *Famouz* – und damit gewissermaßen auch seiner Person –, fällt auf, wie eng sein Leben und seine Arbeit miteinander verflochten sind. Die knappe Sprache, in der Corbijn über sich selbst redet, wirkt ähnlich suggestiv und poetisch wie seine Schwarzweiß-Portraits. Auch der Bericht über seinen Werdegang fällt knapp aus; er ist streng strukturiert, beschränkt sich auf das Wesentliche und lässt der Phantasie des Zuhörers viel Freiraum. Das ganzseitige Selbstportrait in *Famouz* ist in dieser Hinsicht sehr aufschlußreich. Es zeigt

become a portrait photographer? The artistic and commercial success now enjoyed by Anton Corbijn seems to fly in the face of all expectations. Nevertheless he describes himself as an outsider, someone who did not come from an artistic environment, and who with no formal training has a constantly nagging feeling of not knowing enough.

The choices Corbijn made in his youth conjure up the image of the little boy running away from home and heading off into the world – following the band and the circus troupe. Although variations on this unmistakably romantic theme, such as the popular children's book *Alone in the World,* or Fellini's film *La Strada* (a somewhat updated variant), were in circulation way back in the 1950s, this nevertheless remains an unusual role for someone undergoing the stresses of growing up in the 1960s.

Corbijn's work has an undeniable element of adventure. Having stepped into the limelight with the publication of *Famouz,* it becomes apparent for the first time how closely interwoven his life and work are. The sober account Corbijn gives of his own career is as suggestive and poetic as his black-and-white portraits. Like them, his account is tightly constructed, spare in detail, and yet creates a context with scope for the imagination. In that sense the full-page self-portrait he appended to *Famouz* is significant. It has the same stylistic characteristics as the other portraits, but it is striking that his own face remains out-of-focus and that he has blurred his first name, scrawled on the back wall, with a thin stroke of paint.

In conversation with me Corbijn characterized *Famouz* as a boy's dream: 'It's a book about a boy travelling round the world with a camera, meeting people, taking photos, and if there are no people, taking photos of the city he is in. It's the idea of taking off somewhere with your camera and coming back home, developing your stuff in the darkroom – and that's your day's work, your encounter.' This notion makes it clear that the publication of *Famouz* meant an unexpected encounter with himself.

The need for change and for broadening one's base is a constantly recurring motif in our conversation, in such statements as: 'I'm someone who likes to change now and again.' 'I don't really have any grand design

die gleichen stilistischen Merkmale wie die anderen Portraits, doch fällt auf, dass Corbijns Gesicht unscharf bleibt und daß er seinen Vornamen, der auf der Wand hinter ihm geschrieben steht, mit Pinselstrichen fast bis zur Unleserlichkeit verwischt hat.

Corbijn nennt *Famouz* die Verwirklichung eines Kindertraums: „Es ist das Buch eines Jungen, der mit einer Kamera durch die Welt reist, Menschen begegnet und Photos macht, und wenn keine Menschen da sind, macht er ein Photo von der Stadt, in der er gerade ist. Die Idee ist: Man geht mit seiner Kamera irgendwohin, kommt dann wieder nach Hause und entwickelt seine Sachen in der Dunkelkammer. Und das war es dann, was du gemacht hast. Das war deine Begegnung." So gesehen, musste die Veröffentlichung von *Famouz* für ihn zu einer unerwarteten Begegnung auch mit sich selbst werden.

Ein immer wiederkehrendes Thema in unserem Gespräch war das Bedürfnis nach Veränderung und Weiterentwicklung. Das klang etwa so: „Ich bin jemand, der doch hin und wieder Veränderung braucht"; „... ich habe eigentlich kein großes Konzept vor Augen, nur dass ich meine Photographie verändern wollte, als ich das Buch fertig hatte"; „... die Technik hat nur einen geringen Anteil und fällt mir sehr leicht, und deshalb möchte ich auch anderes aus mir herausholen"; „... bei Farbe muss man sich genauer überlegen, was man machen will. Und überhaupt will ich mehr darüber nachdenken, was ein Bild bedeutet." Auch weniger persönliche Überlegungen spielen eine Rolle. Die Frage etwa nach dem Stellenwert, den er als Europäer gegenüber internationalen Größen wie Herb Ritts und Bruce Weber einnimmt. Oder die Tatsache, dass sein Werk in den USA vergleichsweise unbekannt ist, gemessen an seinen Erfolgen in Europa und Japan. Und schließlich das Gefühl, plötzlich zu einer Art Künstler geworden zu sein, obwohl er anfangs keinerlei Ambitionen in dieser Richtung hatte. Fünfzehn Jahre lang waren Hotelzimmer und Flughäfen die Angelpunkte seines Lebens, seiner Arbeit und seiner Sicht der Welt. Corbijn eignete sich in dieser Zeit nicht nur die Fähigkeit an, schnell zu reagieren und kurzfristig zu disponieren, sondern auch eine Weitläufigkeit, die mit jener typisch

in mind, except that I knew I wanted to take a new direction in my work after I finished the book.' 'It's not very technical and comes naturally to me, so that I want to draw on other parts of myself.' 'With colour you have to work more consciously, and I want to force myself to think in more general terms about what makes an image.'

There are other considerations besides personal motivation, such as his position as a European vis-a-vis internationally-known photographers like Herb Ritts and Bruce Weber, the fact that his work remains relatively unknown in the United States compared with his success in Europe and Japan, and the feeling of having suddenly become something of an artist, although that was not initially his ambition. For fifteen years hotel rooms and airports were the jumping-off points for his work and his observations of the world. In this period Corbijn trained himself to develop his ideas in just a few minutes, acquiring an international experience far removed from his cosy childhood world in the Netherlands. He speaks of his need for a permanent base, a house and a place to live besides his work address which, as the co-owner of a video company, he has located in Los Angeles. His choice will in any case no longer be London, where he has lived up to now. He finds England too irritating, and without going into detail mentions short-term thinking and the present bleak gloom. Back to the Netherlands, perhaps?

In striving for a balance between domesticity, quiet and the stimuli he needs for his work, Corbijn is constantly reviewing his options. Distance is no object: his work involves him in a great deal of travel anyway. As we talk, it emerges that not only cities but national cultures too have faces and characters of their own with which he feels at home in varying degrees. Corbijn unconsciously orchestrates his own tension and calm. Just as he contrasts black and white in his photographs, and working with living. The same applies to black-and-white as opposed to colour, or his work in relation to his need for change. Here too the handling of place, time and opportunity reveals the masterly hand of the travelling photographer.

holländischen Häuslichkeit, in der er aufgewachsen war, kaum mehr etwas gemeinsam hat. Jetzt spricht er von dem Bedürfnis, sesshaft zu werden, von einem Haus und einem Ort nur zum Wohnen. Arbeiten wird er hauptsächlich in Los Angeles, dem Firmensitz einer Video Company, deren Miteigentümer er ist. Für London, sein bisheriges Domizil, wird er sich jedenfalls nicht mehr entscheiden. An England irritieren ihn zu viele Dinge – er erwähnt, ohne weiter ins Detail zu gehen, das Denken ohne langfristige Perspektiven und die bedrückende Enge. Vielleicht doch wieder Holland?

Als es darum geht, seine Vorstellung von Gleichgewicht zwischen dem Bedürfnis nach Ruhe und den für seine Arbeit notwendigen Stimulanzien näher zu definieren, werden Corbijns Denkmuster nach und nach deutlicher. Entfernung spielt keine Rolle; sein Beruf setzt voraus, dass er viel reist. Es zeigt sich, dass nicht nur Städte, sondern auch nationale Kulturen für ihn ein bestimmtes Gesicht, einen bestimmten Charakter haben, der ihm mehr oder auch weniger zusagt. Die Art, wie er Momente der Spannung und der Ruhe in sich selbst zum Ausgleich zu bringen versucht, fast unbewusst, entspricht der – bewussten – Inszenierung des Verhältnisses von Schwarz und Weiß in seinen Photographien. Arbeiten und häusliches Leben stellt er einander gegenüber wie das Schwarzweiß der Farbe; unter demselben Aspekt spielt er die Arbeit und sein Bedürfnis nach Veränderung gegeneinander aus. Und seine Bilder, photographische Verdichtungen von Ort, Zeit und Möglichkeiten, belegen schließlich den Anspruch des ständig Reisenden auf Vollkommenheit.

Es fällt auf, dass sich die Kunst- und die Musikszene bei der ästhetischen Vermarktung ihres Talentpotentials unterschiedlicher Methoden bedienen. In der Regel verursacht das keine Verwirrung, denn beide Bereiche haben ihre jeweils eigene Definition von Professionalität und ihre jeweils eigene Bildersprache. Sobald aber die Grenzen überschritten werden und die fachspezifischen Kriterien der visuellen Umsetzung formuliert werden sollen, tauchen Probleme auf.

Folglich stellt sich auch in diesem Zusammenhang die Frage nach möglichen Bezügen zum Werk anderer Photographen. Mit anderen Worten:

Oddly enough, the artistic and musical worlds have relatively few points of contact in their artistic and public channelling of talent. That usually causes no confusion, as both disciplines have their own professional standards, and both in pop music and in the visual arts there is a recognizable visual culture. However, when lines of demarcation are crossed and criteria have to be formulated affecting differing professional values, there is in essence a conflict.

Here too then we need to ask whether and how Corbijn's work can be related to that of other photographers. In other words, does his work stand in a photographic tradition? Or is the photo good if the designer of the front page says it is?

On the one hand it could be argued that Corbijn's portraits are so specifically tailored to the associative use of images that, in video clips and in the illustrative and P. R. material used by pop groups, they seem to stand up as such in their own right. Yet there is more to be said about his method. Corbijn omits certain things that were used, for example, by American photographers such as Avedon and Penn in an earlier generation, by Mapplethorpe, and now by Ritts and Weber. He does not isolate his subjects from their background, does not neutralize the latter and uses no backdrops. On the contrary, backgrounds have a clear and active function, regardless of whether that background is a landscape, a symbolic context, or an abstract sculpture in light and shadow. Corbijn is not content with a vague indication of place as context but adheres to the theatrical unity of time, place and action. Consequently his photos have a rhythmic structure akin to documentary photography. This contrasts with the work of American colleagues, which aims first and foremost at monumentality, subscribing as it does to the principles of fashion and glamour photography. Anton Corbijn works more with character than with physical beauty. He pays no attention in his work to elegance or the texture of skin or clothing. Not even when photographing David Bowie, for example (Chicago 1980), or Siouxie Sioux (Kyoto 1982), both semi-nude, or the face of Peter Hammill (Bath 1986) in close-up, where his main concern is the expression of

beruht die Qualität von Corbijns Arbeiten auf einer photographischen Tradition, oder ist ein Photo dann gut, wenn es der Coverdesigner für verwertbar hält?

Man könnte die These vertreten, Corbijns Portraits seien dem assoziativen Stil der Video-Clips verpflichtet, diesem spezifischen visuellen PR-Produkt der Popindustrie; sie würden demnach eine eigenständige photographische Gattung repräsentieren. Doch beinhaltet die Art seines Photographierens mehr. Corbijn verzichtet beispielsweise auf eine Reihe von Stilelementen, die von amerikanischen Photographen erfolgreich eingesetzt wurden; früher von Avedon und Penn, dann von Mapplethorpe und heute von Ritts und Weber. Corbijn isoliert seine Sujets nicht; bei ihm gibt es weder neutralisierte Hintergründe noch sogenannte „backdrops" – letztlich künstliche Versatzstücke, Kulissen. Der Hintergrund hat bei Corbijn eine deutlich aktive Funktion, gleichgültig ob es sich um eine Landschaft, einen symbolischen Kontext oder eine aus Licht und Schatten abstrahierte Struktur handelt. Corbijn begnügt sich nicht mit vagen Andeutungen, er hält konsequent an der dramaturgischen Einheit von Ort, Zeit und Handlung fest. Seine Bilder wirken dadurch rhythmisch komponiert und fast wie Dokumentaraufnahmen – ganz im Gegensatz zur Ästhetik seiner amerikanischen Kollegen, die den Prinzipien der Mode- und Glamourphotographie folgt und in erster Linie monumental sein will.

Corbijn arbeitet mit Charakteren, weniger mit physischer Schönheit. Der sinnlichen Eleganz oder der Textur von Haut und Kleidung schenkt er kaum Beachtung; auch dann nicht, wenn er David Bowie (Chicago, 1980) und Siouxsie Sioux (Kyoto, 1982) mit nacktem Oberkörper oder das Gesicht von Peter Hammill (Bath, 1986) in Nahaufnahme photographiert. Auch hier geht es ihm primär um den Ausdruck eines Charakters und die Bedeutung einer Form. Sein Sinn für Schönheit steht nicht isoliert für sich; die anatomische Erotik einzelner Körperteile interessiert ihn ebensowenig wie die glatte Virtuosität, mit der sie photographisch erfasst werden kann. Corbijns Portraits handeln von der Existenz, jener anderen, vielleicht abendländischeren Dimension von Schönheit. Und sie handeln von Freundschaft:

character and the significance of form. His sense of beauty is not something autonomous, nor is he interested in the erotic anatomy of physical shapes, or the polished virtuosity with which they can be shot. Corbijn's portraits are about human existence, that other, perhaps more European expression of beauty. At the same time they are also sympathetic portraits in which understanding translates apparent social maladjustment into character.

Significant in this respect is the photo he took in 1986 of what was probably a hanging sign for a movie theatre in New York *(People,* New York 1986). The words 'burlesque' and 'joy, friendship, peace' are placed in large illuminated lettering above the series of similarly lit portraits of old-time film stars. The symbolism evoked is one of nostalgia, recalling the one-time greats of the silver screen. The innocence of the past stands in stark contrast to today's scars, like those etched into Billy Idol by the shadow of the letters daubed on his naked torso (Los Angeles 1990): 'Nobody's Fool'. The poetry has a grim quality, which stands in sharp contrast with society's belief in well-being – Corbijn photographed the careworn face of Joe Cocker (The Hague 1979) in front of the Eldorado beach cafe. With Corbijn even Marianne Faithfull (Los Angeles, 1990) has exchanged the romantic beauty captured by Mapplethorpe and others for a more contemporary look, bearing the traces of tension and weariness.

Mention should certainly be made in this connection of the work of Helmut Newton, and specifically his portrait of Marianne Faithfull clad only in a black bra. Newton was the first European to inject an audacity new to the American public into glamour photography. And if one is to close the circle of links within the Western hemisphere, on the American side Mapplethorpe's series of portraits of the then young rock singer Patti Smith should not be forgotten. However, with both Newton and Mapplethorpe, even in the portraits just quoted, the pose of the subject has a different significance.

Looking for photographers with some similarity to Corbijn in their work settings, one is more inclined to think of someone like Robert Frank and his hard, poetic images which are in some ways uncomfortable to live with

seine Sympathie und sein Verständnis für offenkundige gesellschaftliche Unangepasstheit setzt Corbijn direkt in Bilder von individuell ausgeprägten Persönlichkeiten um.

Aufschlussreich ist in diesem Zusammenhang ein Photo von einem Reklameschild, 1986 offenbar vor einem New Yorker Kino entstanden (*People,* New York, 1986). In großen leuchtenden Lettern stehen die Worte „burlesk" und „joy, friendship, peace" über einer Reihe ebenfalls angestrahlter Portraits alter Filmstars. Die heraufbeschworene Symbolik hat etwas Nostalgisches; es ist eine wehmütige Erinnerung an die Leinwandstars von gestern – und an die Unschuld vergangener Zeiten. Denn der Kontrast zum Heute ist scharf und unübersehbar; wie Narben einer eingeätzten Tätowierung steht es auf Billy Idols Brust (Los Angeles, 1990) geschrieben: „Nobody's Fool", die Schatten von irgendwo hingeschmierten Buchstaben. Die Poesie ist grimmiger geworden; auf den zähen Wohlstandsglauben der Gesellschaft reagiert sie mit zunehmender Heftigkeit. Corbijn photographierte das zerfurchte Gesicht Joe Cockers (Den Haag, 1979) vor einer Strandhütte, die den Namen Eldorado trägt. Und Marianne Faithfull (Los Angeles, 1990) tauscht bei ihm ihre romantische Schönheit, die wir unter anderem von Mapplethorpe-Portraits her kennen, gegen ein weniger idealisiertes Erscheinungsbild ein, das Spuren von Nervosität und Müdigkeit zeigt.

In diesem Zusammenhang sollte Helmut Newton zumindest erwähnt werden, insbesondere sein Portrait von Marianne Faithfull, die für ihn in einem schwarzen BH posierte. Newton, der Europäer, hat als erster das Element der Respektlosigkeit, eigentlich der Frivolität in die Glamour-Photographie eingeführt, für das damalige amerikanische Publikum etwas völlig Fremdes, das jedoch schnell Schule machte.

Will man den Kreis der westlichen Kontinente an diesem Punkt schließen, darf auf amerikanischer Seite Mapplethorpes Portraitserie der jungen Patti Smith nicht fehlen. Allerdings hat die Pose für Mapplethorpe wie für Newton eine Bedeutung, die von Corbijns Auffassung des Portraits grundverschieden ist.

because of their irritant quality. 'Gritty' is the word used by Corbijn to describe his own work. Behind the scenes and between shows, Corbijn makes authentic portraits of the idols. The spotlights or studio lamps are replaced by less flattering but more realistic daylight. In Corbijn's work light has not only a demystifying but also a poetic function. As a 'black black-and-white photographer', as Ron Kaal called him in his review of *Famouz* in relation to Herb Ritts (the white black-and-white photographer), he not only leaves room in the shadows for suggestion and imagination but uses his blacks and greys as abstract forms.

Abstraction is even more pronounced in his colour photography. The juxtaposition of light and dark colours creates a visually interpreted sense of depth, which appears to operate in a similar way but in fact is easier to handle than in black-and-white contrasts. In addition Corbijn also uses colour as an alienating device, as is often done in staged photography, in video clips and record sleeves. Although his colour work still bears marked traces of experiment, it is freer and more playful than his black-and-white oeuvre and in that sense is an enrichment. The leitmotif is again his fascination for pop music and its appeal to the imagination. The intriguing picture of the king in a deckchair from his last video clip for *Depeche Mode* embodies more than pure imagination and carries the implicit message: 'bohemian or king, forever new and young'.

Wenn es Photographen gegeben hat, die in ihrer schöpferischen Haltung eine gewisse Ähnlichkeit mit Corbijn aufweisen, so wäre am ehesten an jemanden wie Robert Frank zu denken. Harte, poetische Bilder, mit denen sich schwer leben lässt, weil sie irritieren. „Gritty“ – sandig, spröde – ist das Wort, das Corbijn benutzt, um sein eigenes Werk zu charakterisieren. Seine Portraits von Idolen entstehen hinter den Kulissen und zwischen den Auftritten. Das Licht der Scheinwerfer oder der Atelierlampen ersetzt er durch das weniger schmeichelnde, aber realistischere Tageslicht.

Das Licht hat in Corbijns Bildern zweifellos eine entmystifizierende Funktion, gleichzeitig aber auch eine poetische. Ron Kaal bezeichnete Corbijn in seiner Rezension von *Famouz* als „schwarzen Schwarzweiß-Photographen“ und setzte ihn damit von Herb Ritts, dem „weißen Schwarzweiß-Photographen“, ab. Tatsächlich bieten Corbijns Schatten der Suggestion und der Phantasie reichen Spielraum, die Ausdrucksskala seiner Schwarz- und Grautöne reicht bis zur äußersten Abstraktion.

Abstraktion ist auch das Schlüsselwort für Corbijns Farbphotographie. Helle und dunkle Farben stellt er einander so gegenüber, dass eine Tiefenwirkung entsteht, die ausschließlich visuell erfassbar wird. Das funktioniert ähnlich wie in seinen Schwarzweiß-Aufnahmen, nur lassen sich Farbkontraste noch effektiver manipulieren und differenzieren. Gleichzeitig setzt er die Farbe in Anlehnung an die Stilmittel der inszenierten Photographie, der Video-Clips und des Plattencover-Designs als verfremdendes Element ein. Corbijns Farbphotographie trägt noch deutlich die Spuren des Experiments, vom Ansatz her ist sie aber freier und spielerischer als seine Schwarzweiß-Technik und insofern eine Bereicherung. Das Leitmotiv ist auch hier die Faszination an der Popmusik und ihre unschätzbare Eigenschaft, die Phantasie anzuregen.

Ein König im Strandkorb – dieses Bild aus Corbijns jüngstem VideoClip für Depeche Mode ist mehr als ein guter Gag oder pure Phantasie. Es enthält die Botschaft: „Bohemien or King, new and young forever.“

TAFELN / PLATES

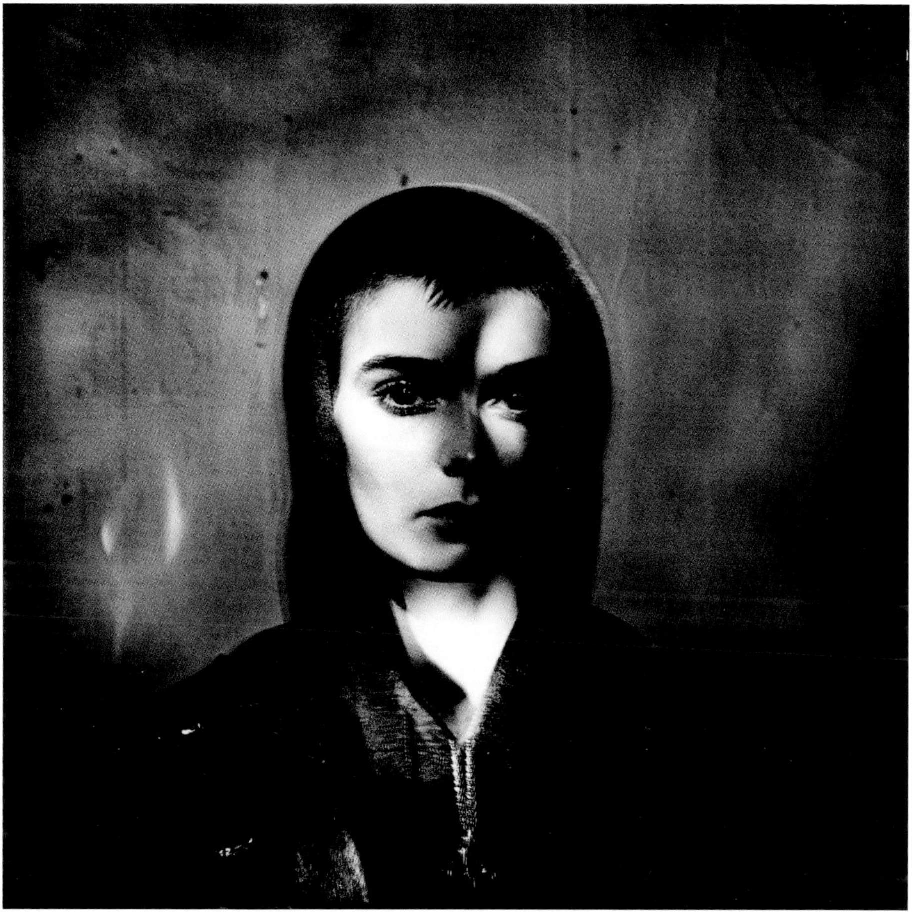

1 SINÉAD O'CONNOR, DUBLIN, 1990

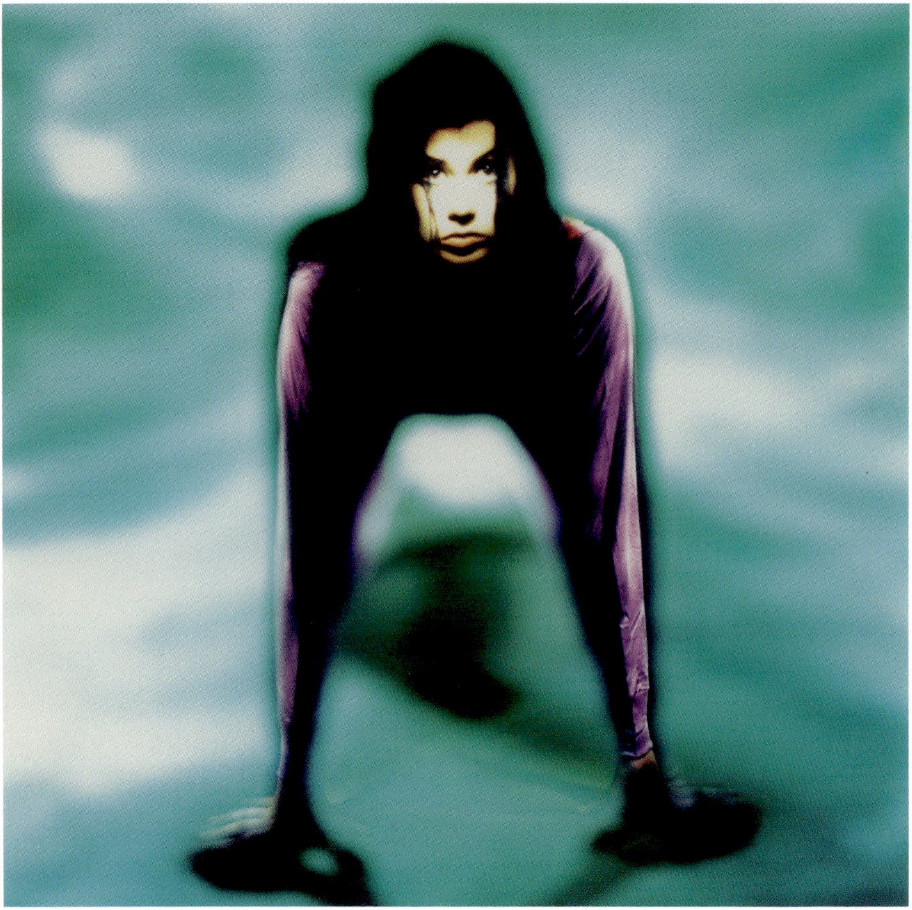

2 TANYA, LONDON, 1990

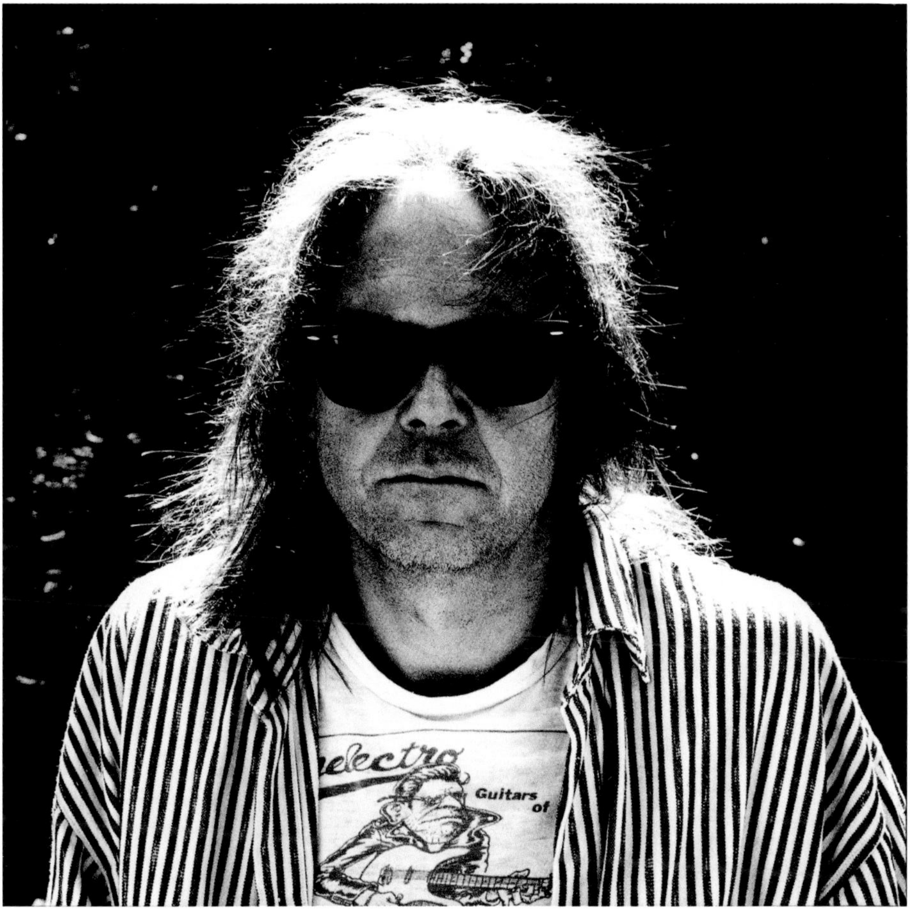

3 NEIL YOUNG, HALF MOON BAY, CA, 1990

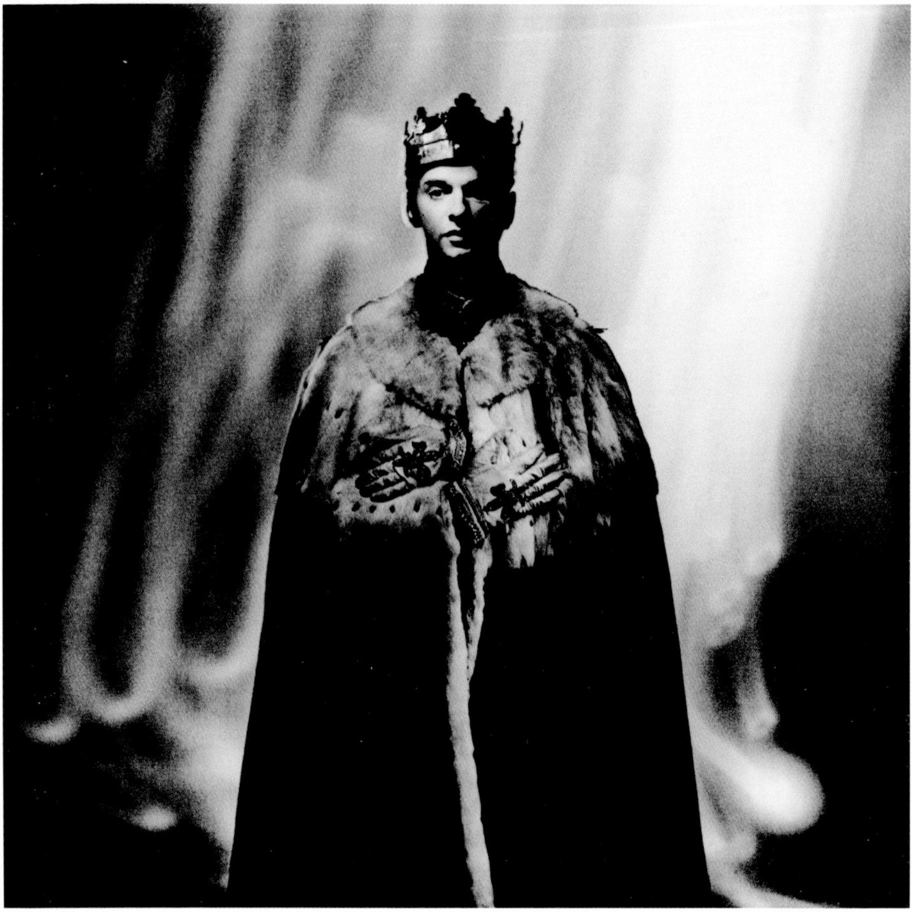

4 DAVE GAHAN (DEPECHE MODE), LONDON, 1989

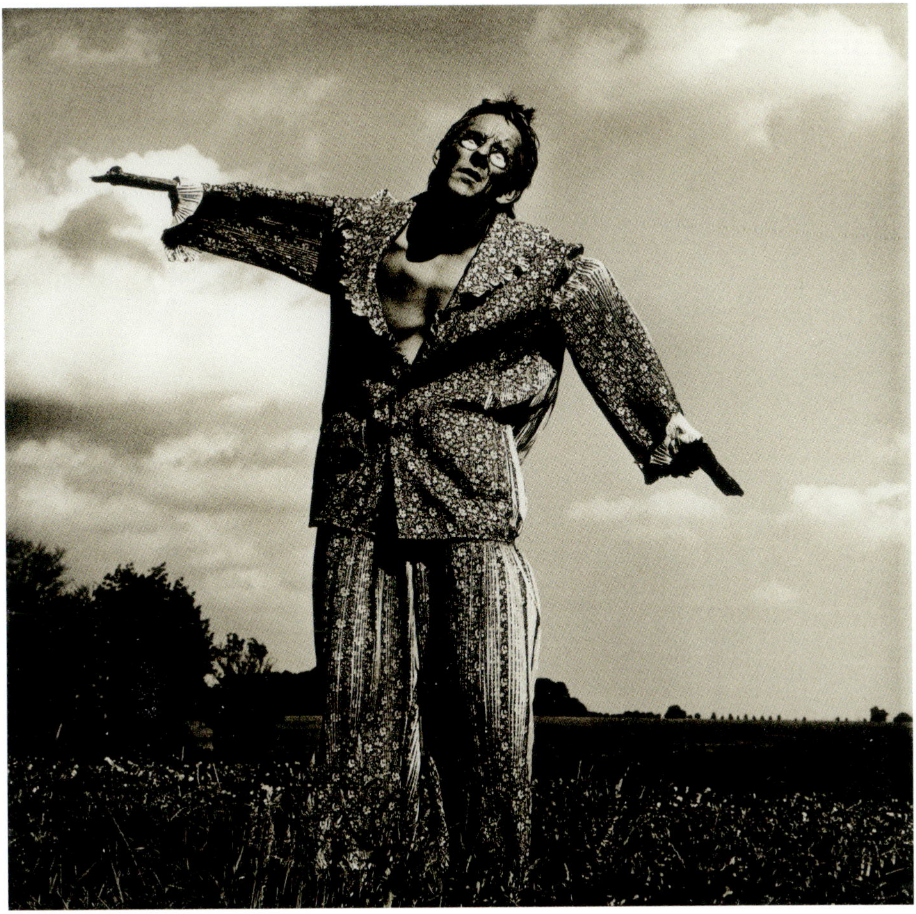

5 FREEK DE JONGE, DEBENHAM, 1989

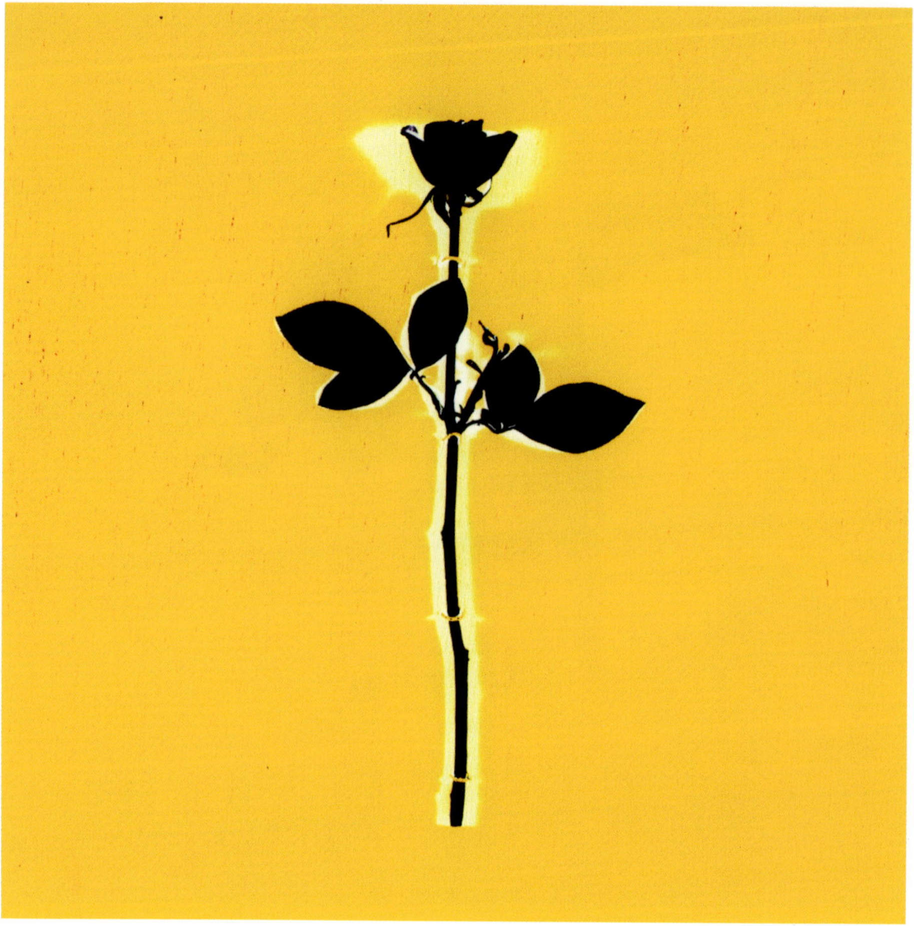

6 ENJOY THE SILENCE, LONDON, 1989

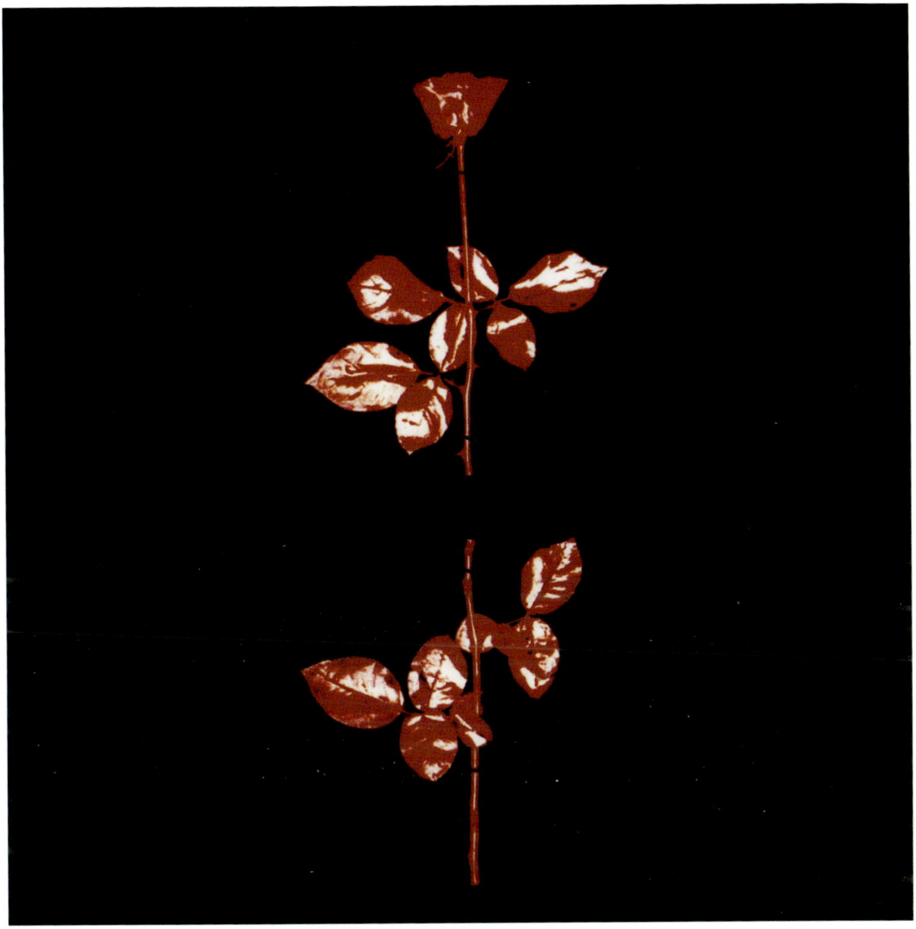

2 VIOLATOR, LONDON, 1989

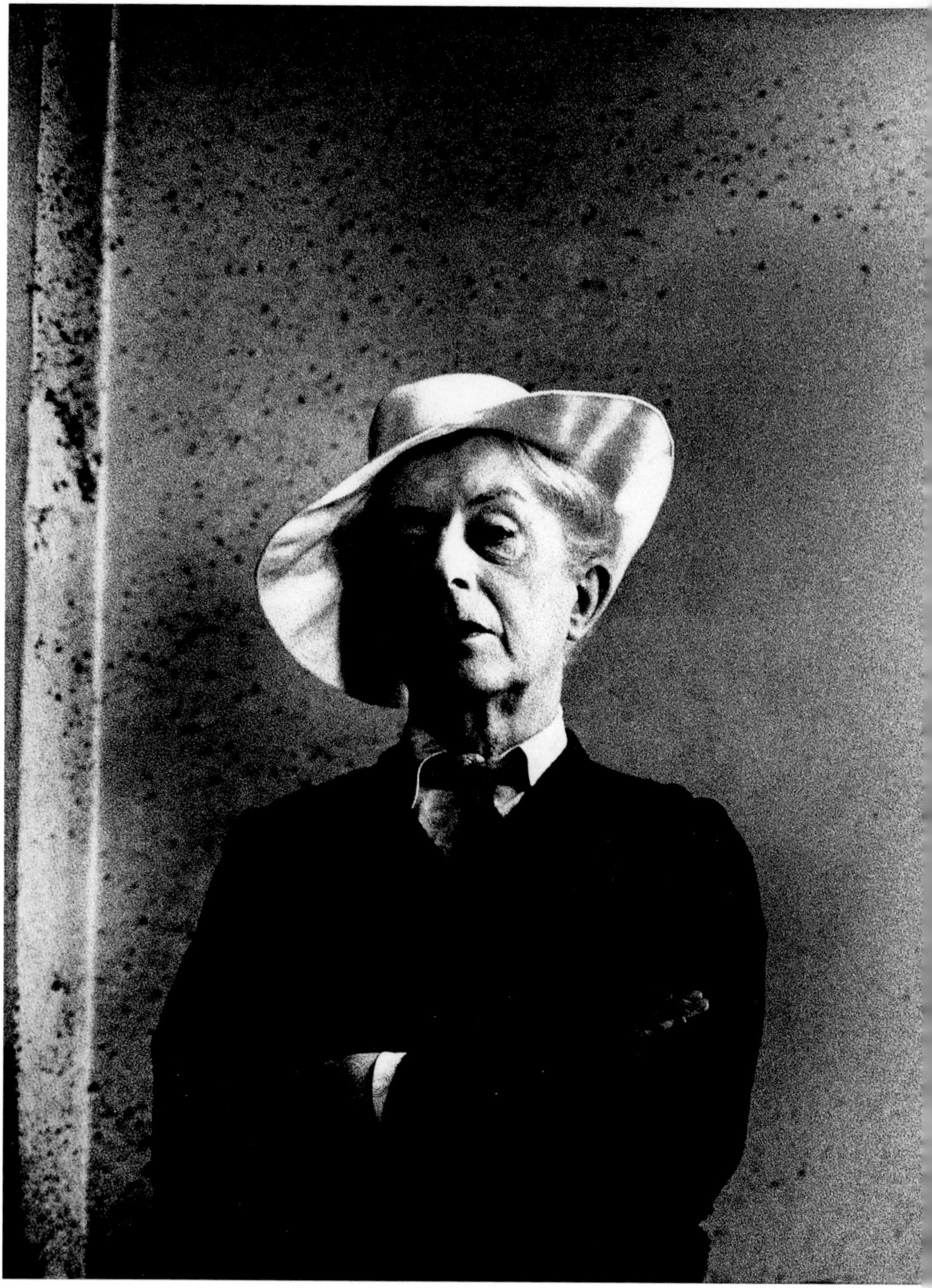

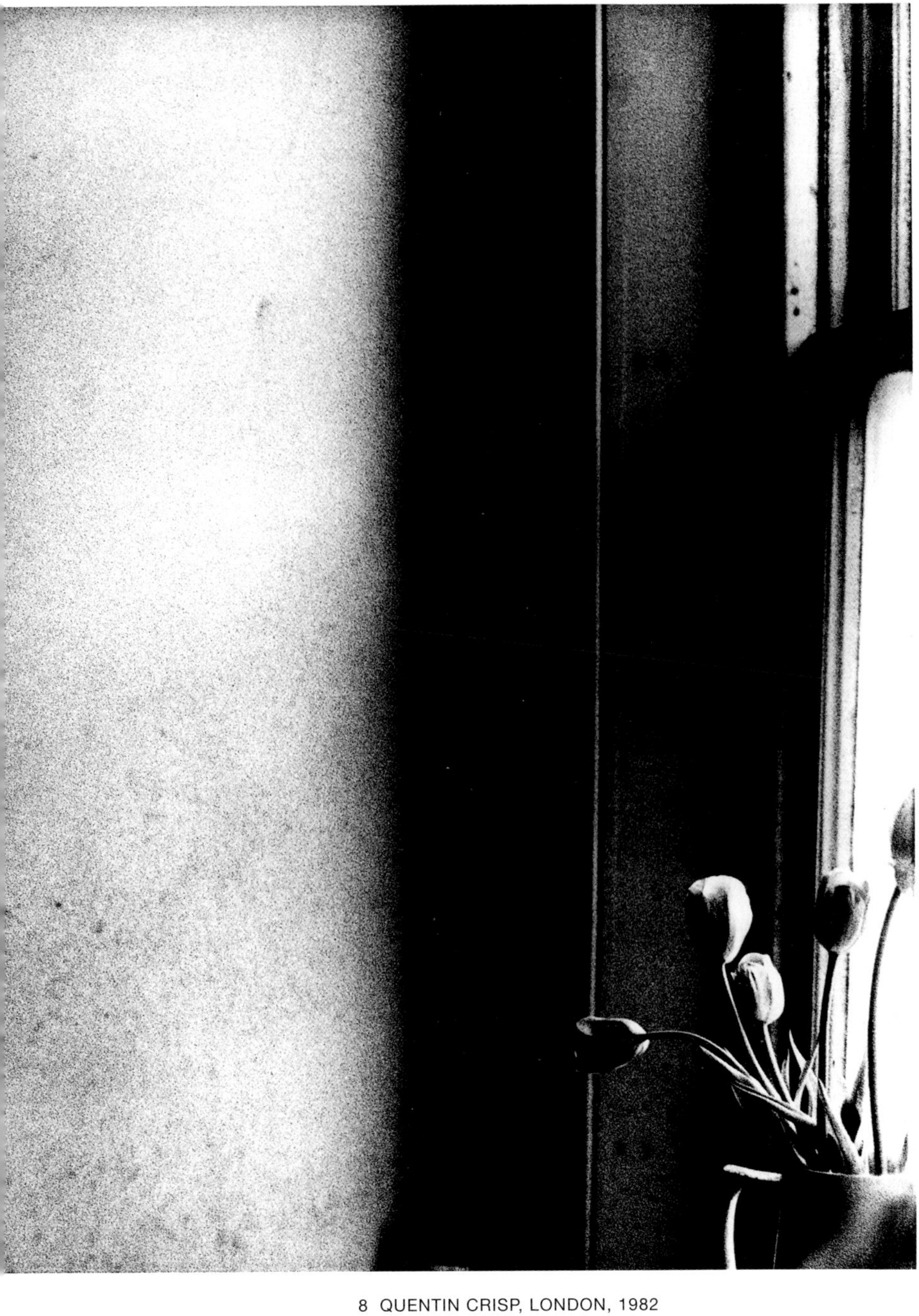

8 QUENTIN CRISP, LONDON, 1982

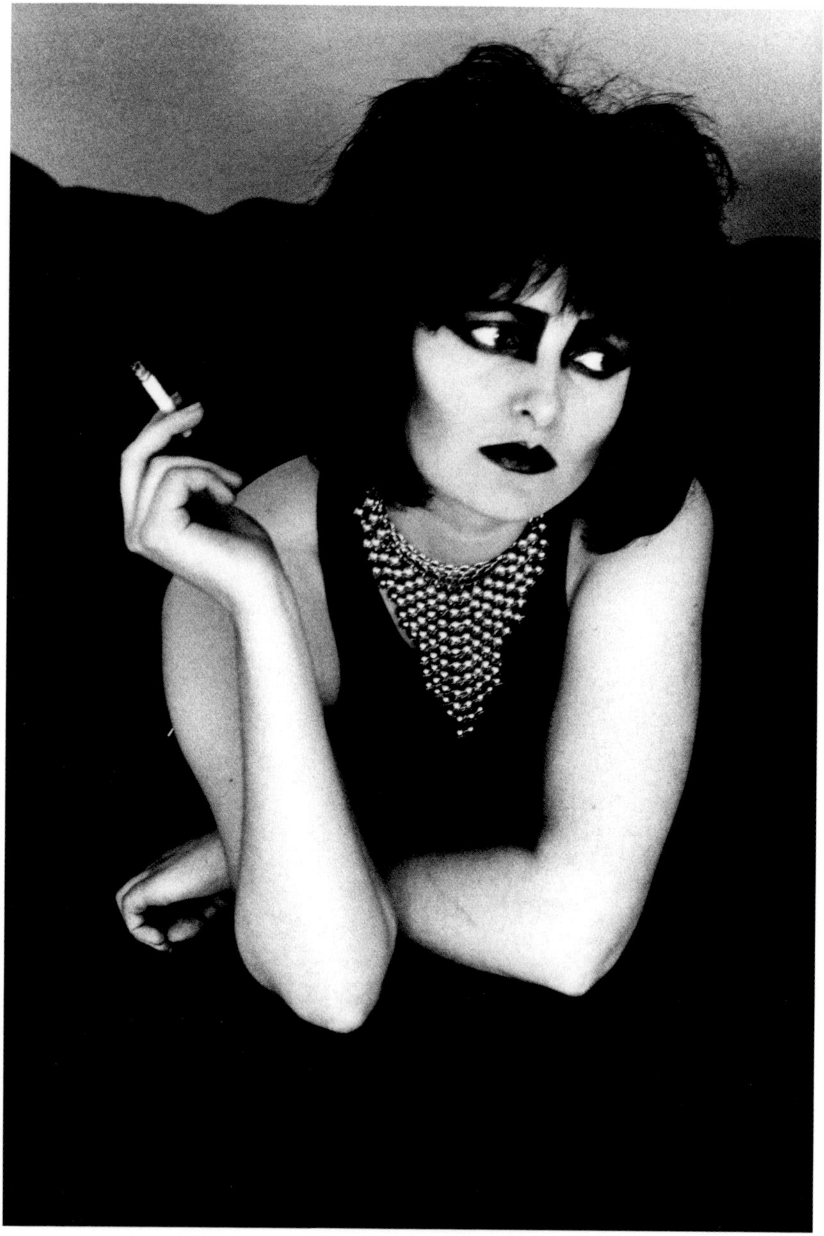

9 SIOUXSIE SIOUX, LONDON, 1985

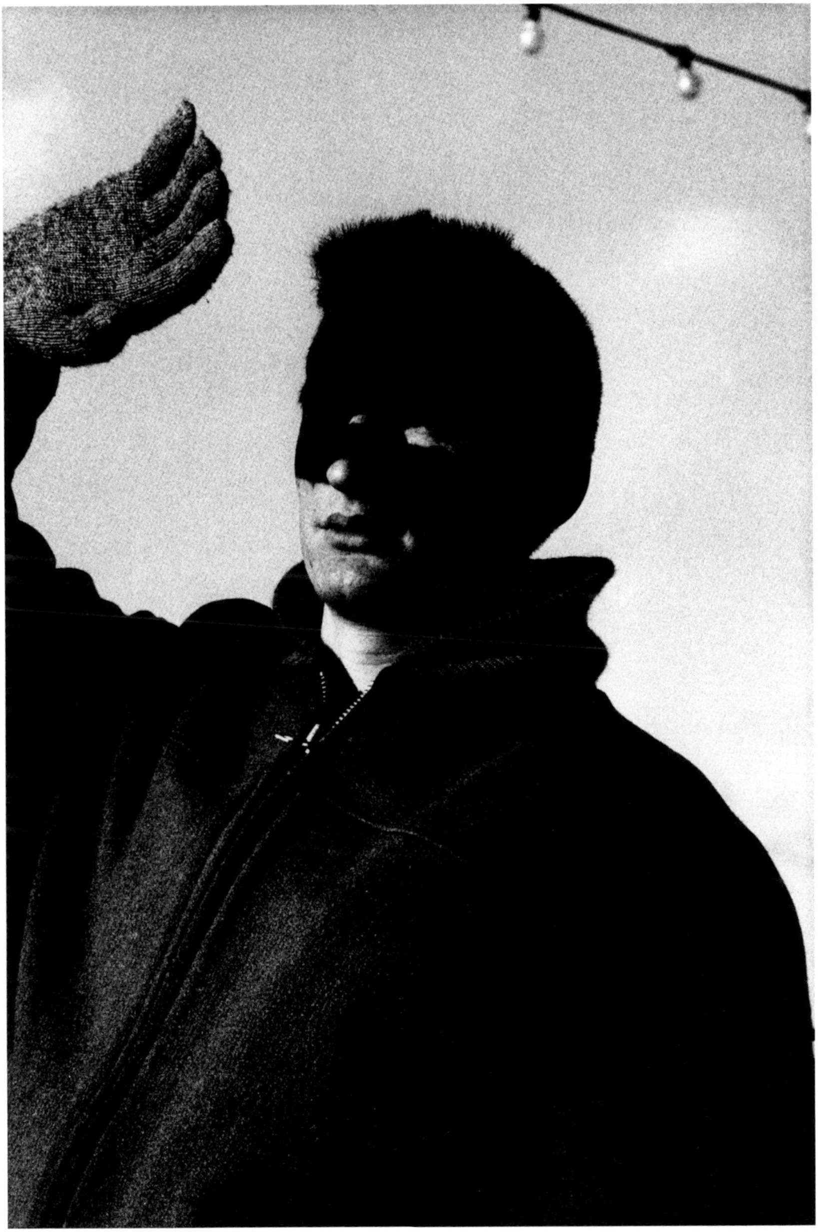

10 BILLY BRAGG, LONDON, 1984

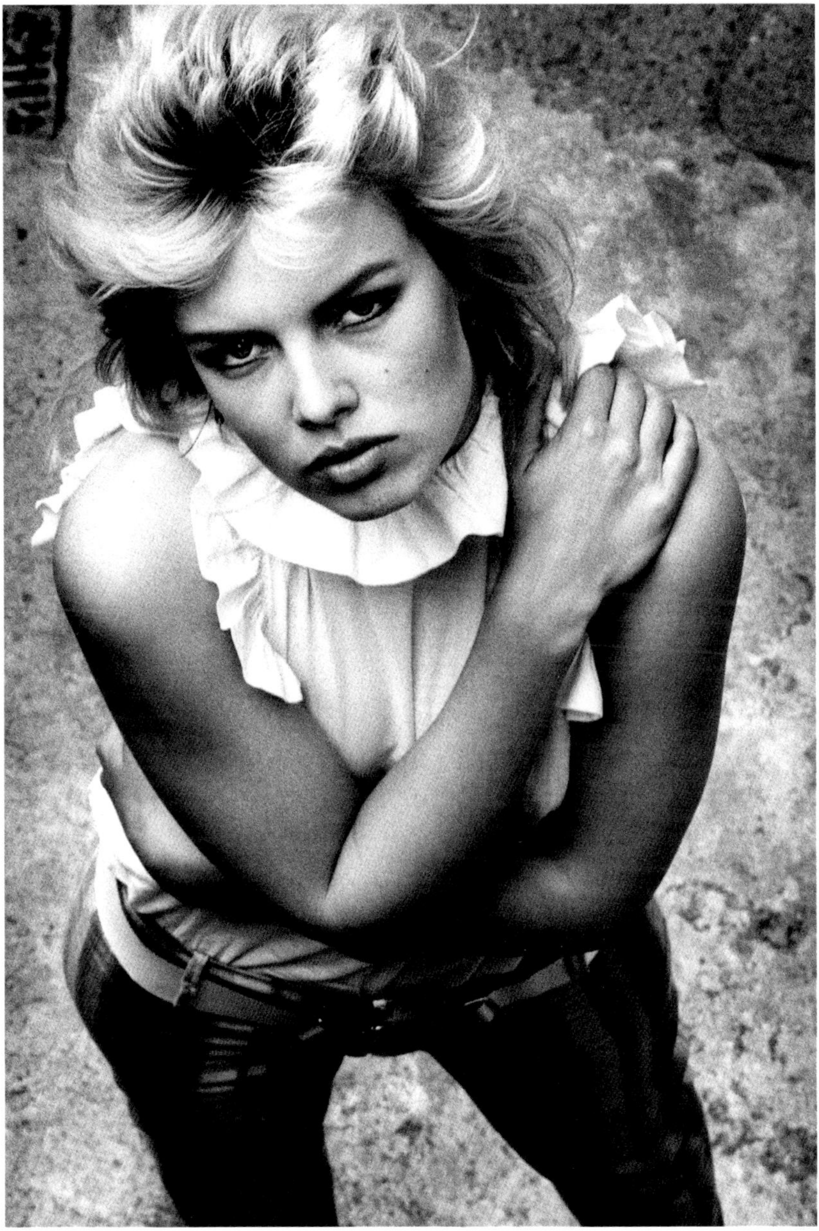

11 KIM WILDE, LONDON, 1980

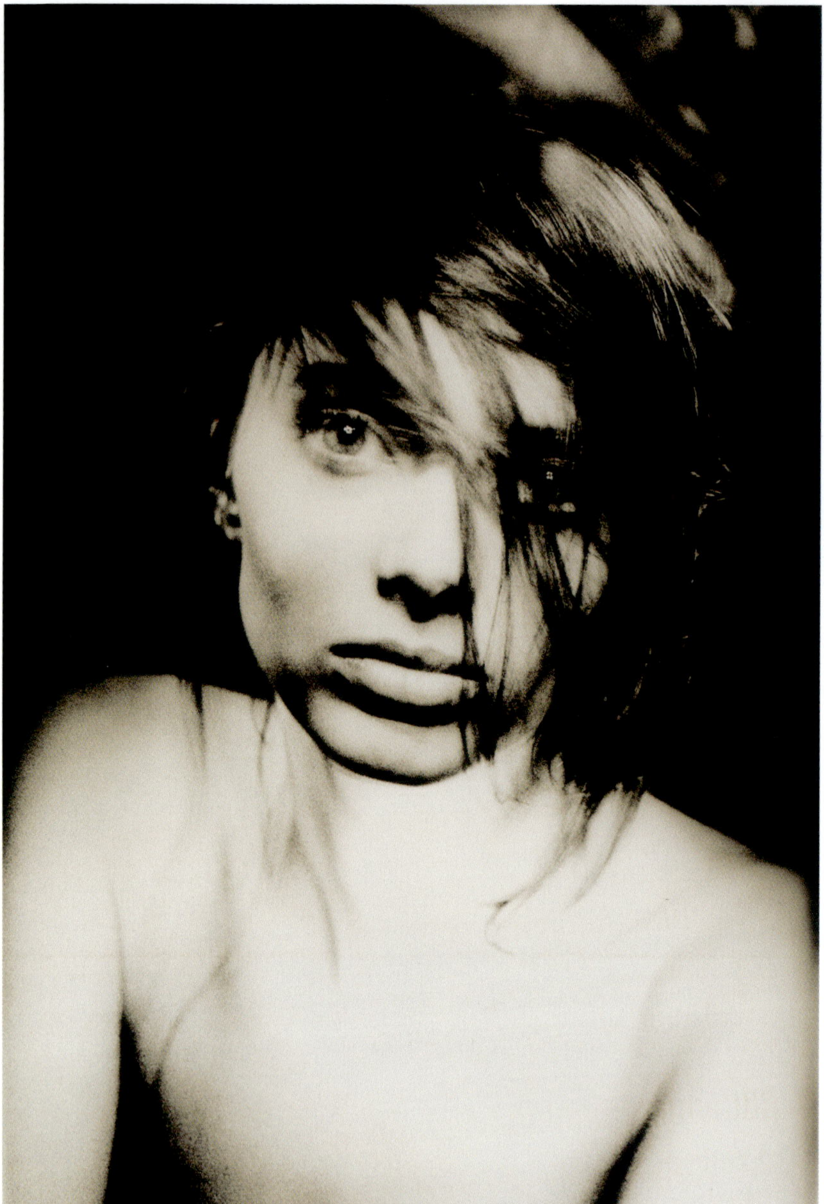

12 HEATHER, LONDON, 1989

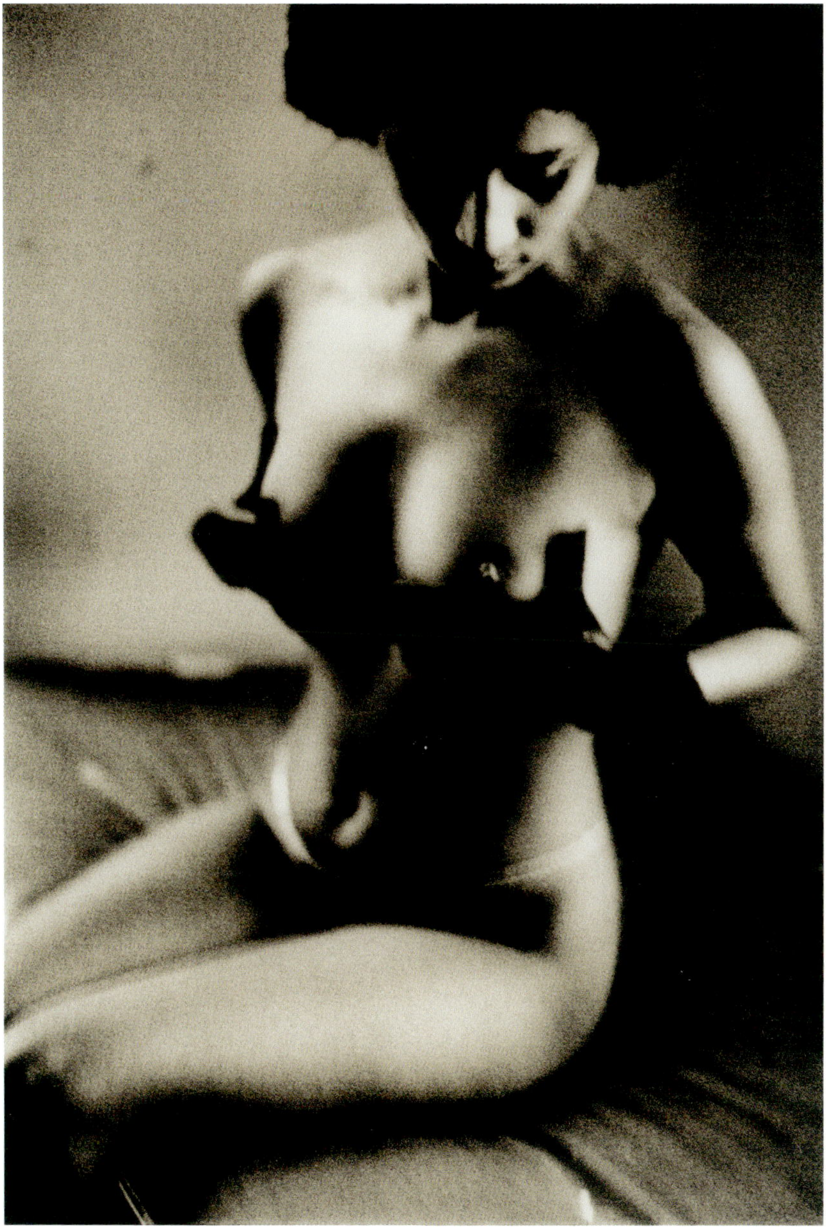

13 NASSIM, LONDON, 1987

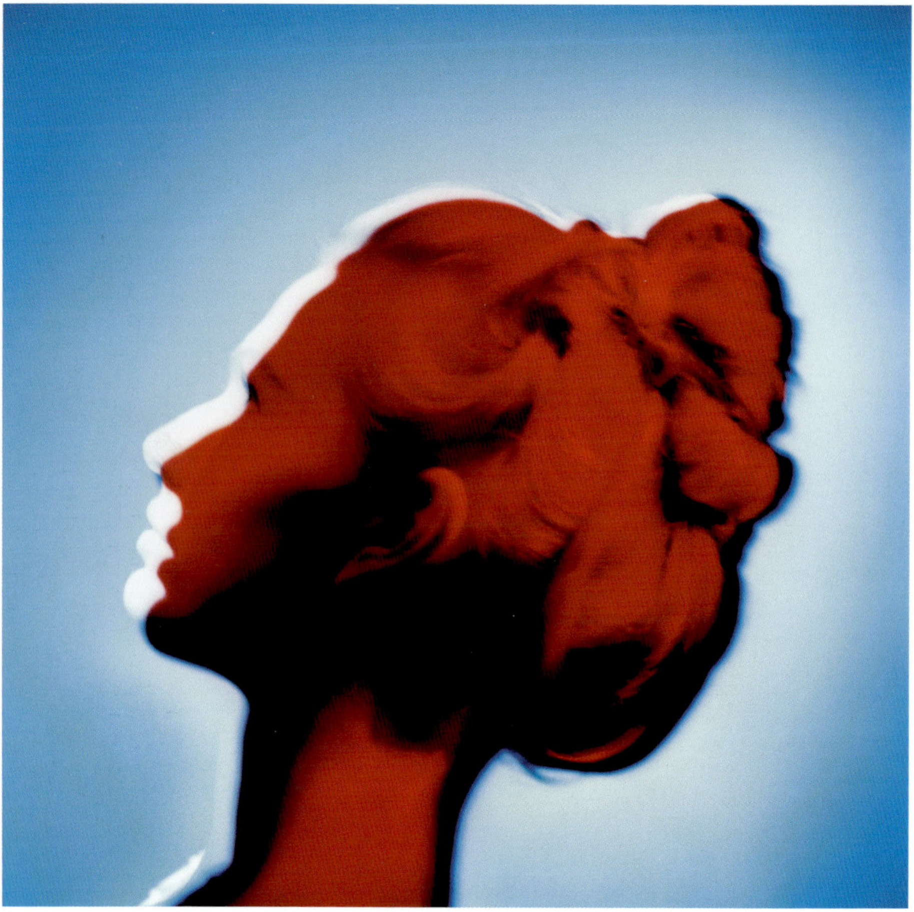

14 PAM, LOS ANGELES, 1990

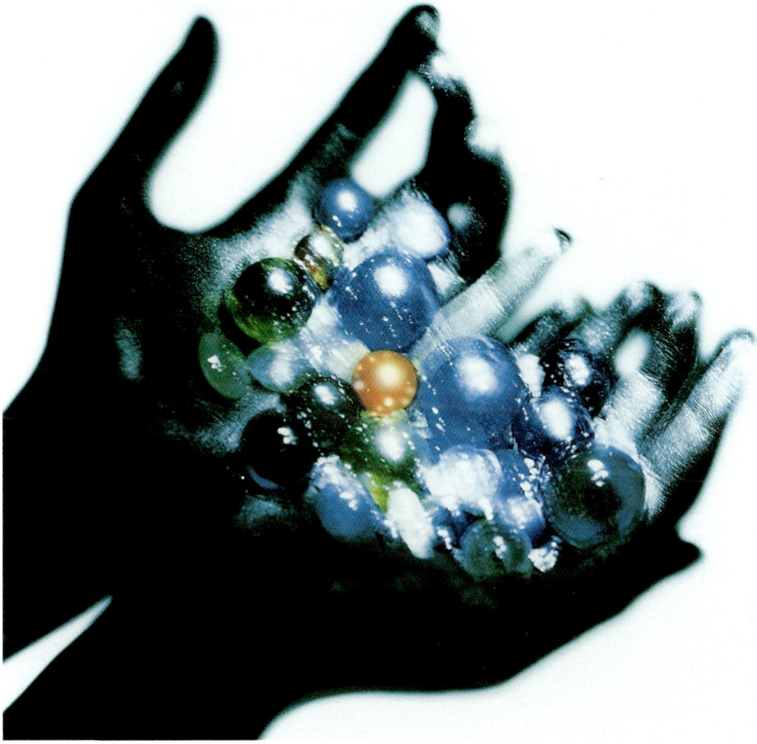

15 ORANGE, LONDON, 1990

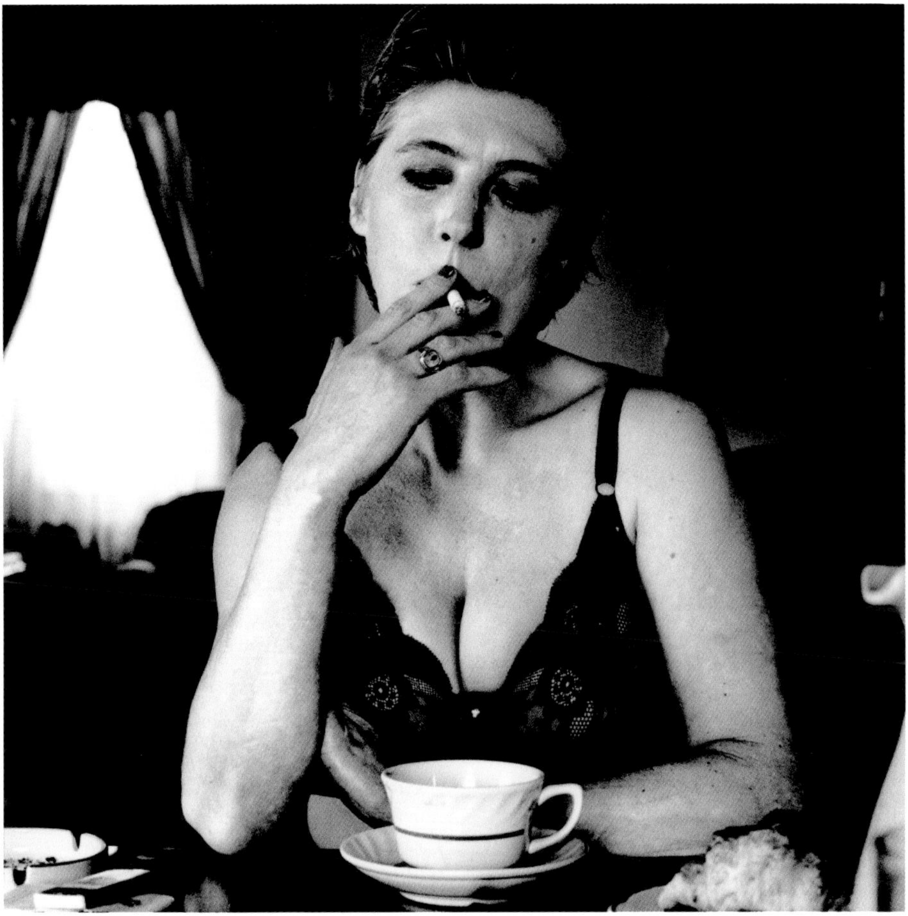

16 MARIANNE FAITHFULL, LOS ANGELES, 1990

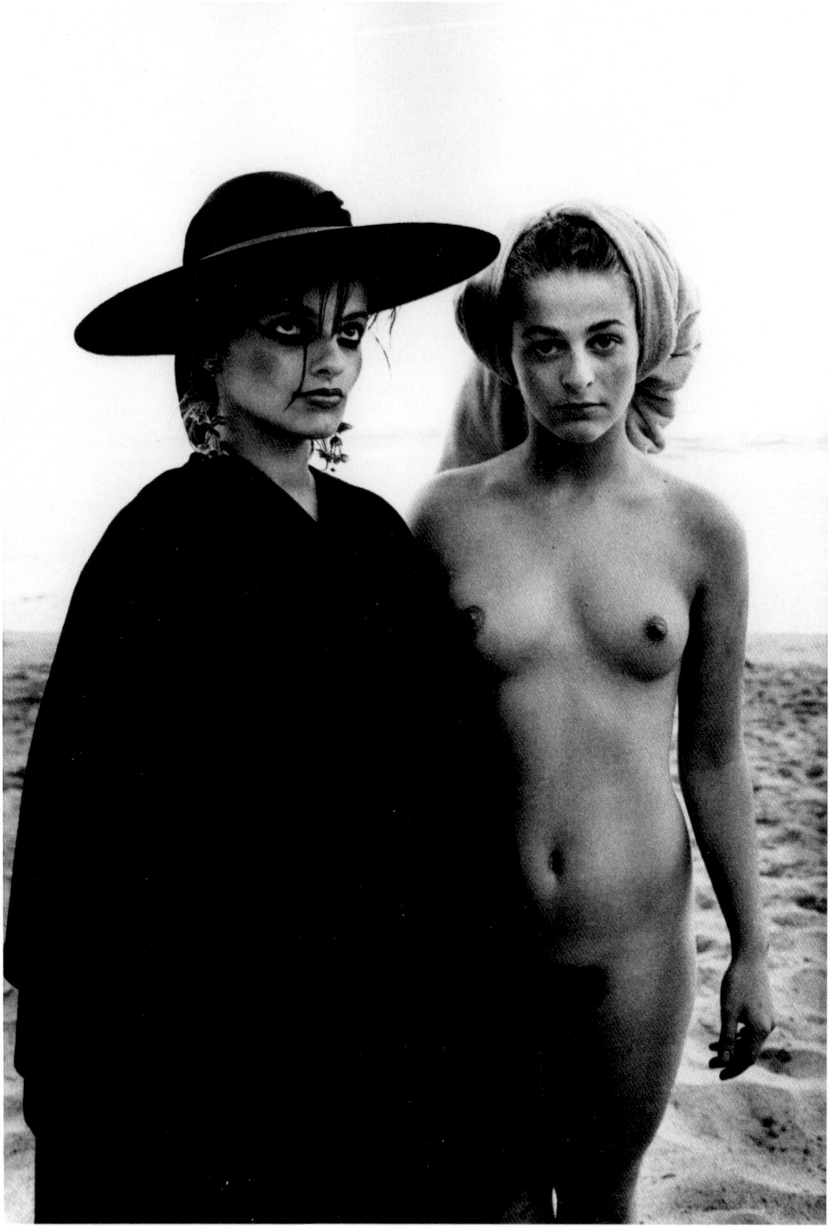

17 NINA HAGEN & ARI UP, MALIBU, 1980

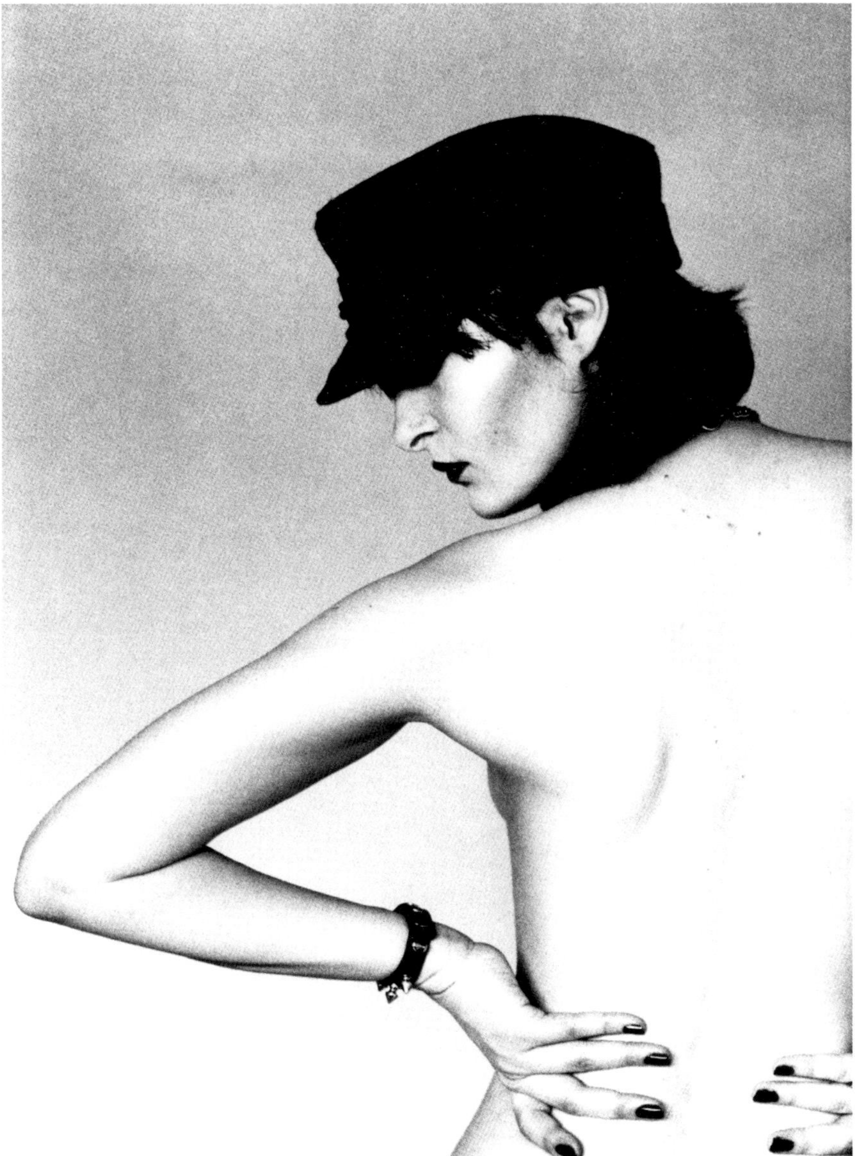

18 SIOUXSIE SIOUX, KYOTO, 1982

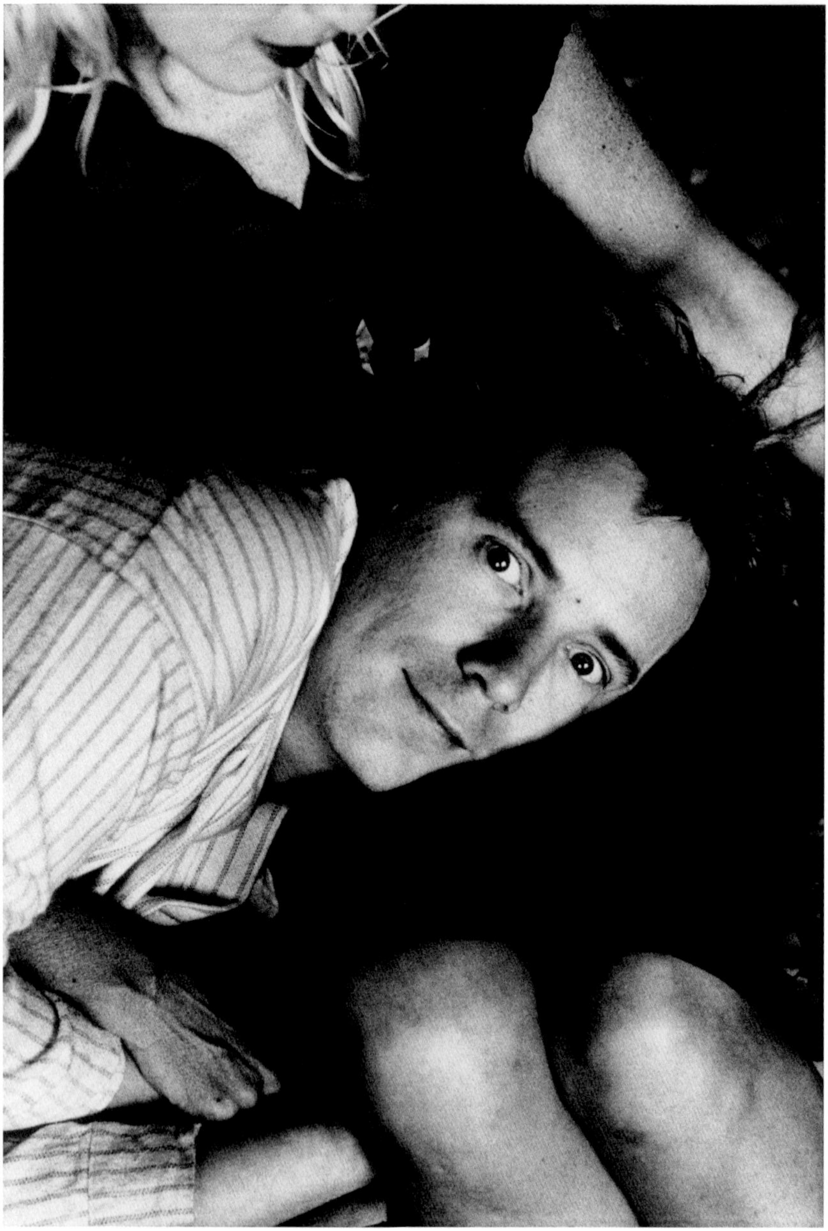

19 JOHN & NORA LYDON, LONDON, 1986

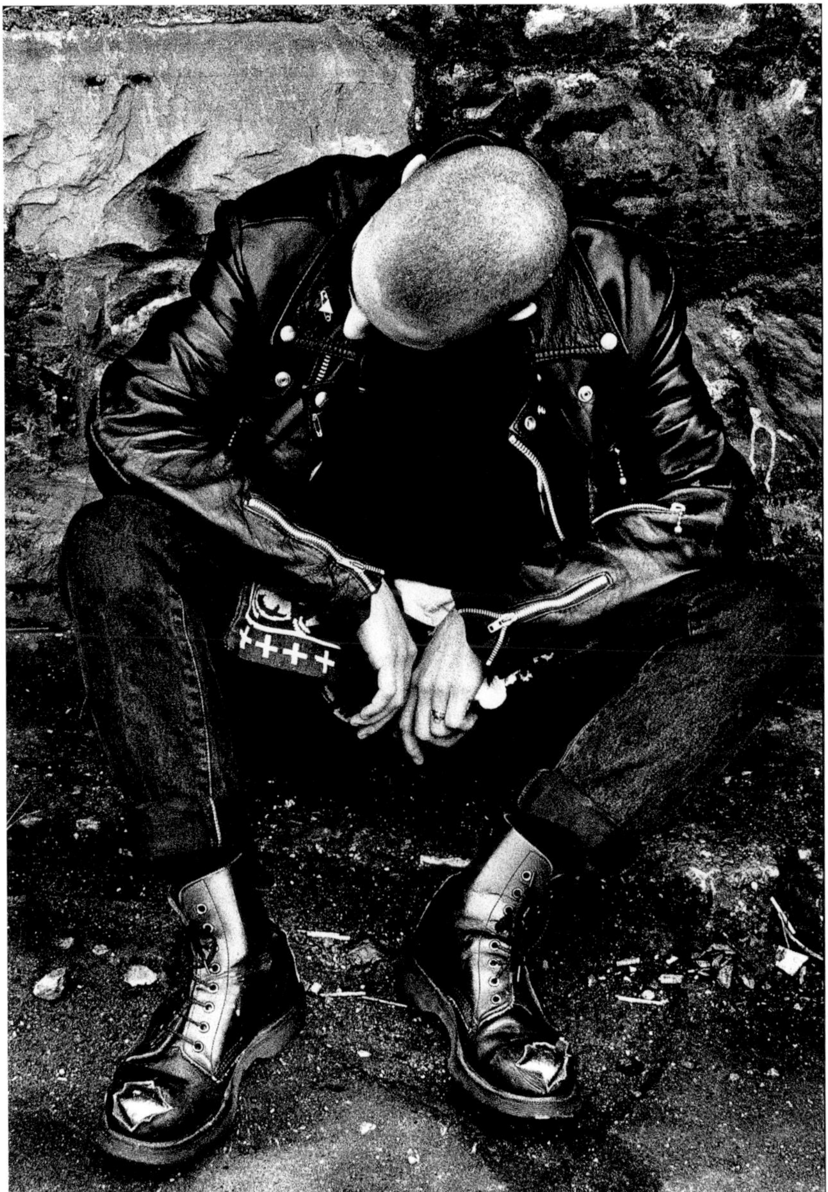

20 SINÉAD O'CONNOR, DUBLIN, 1988

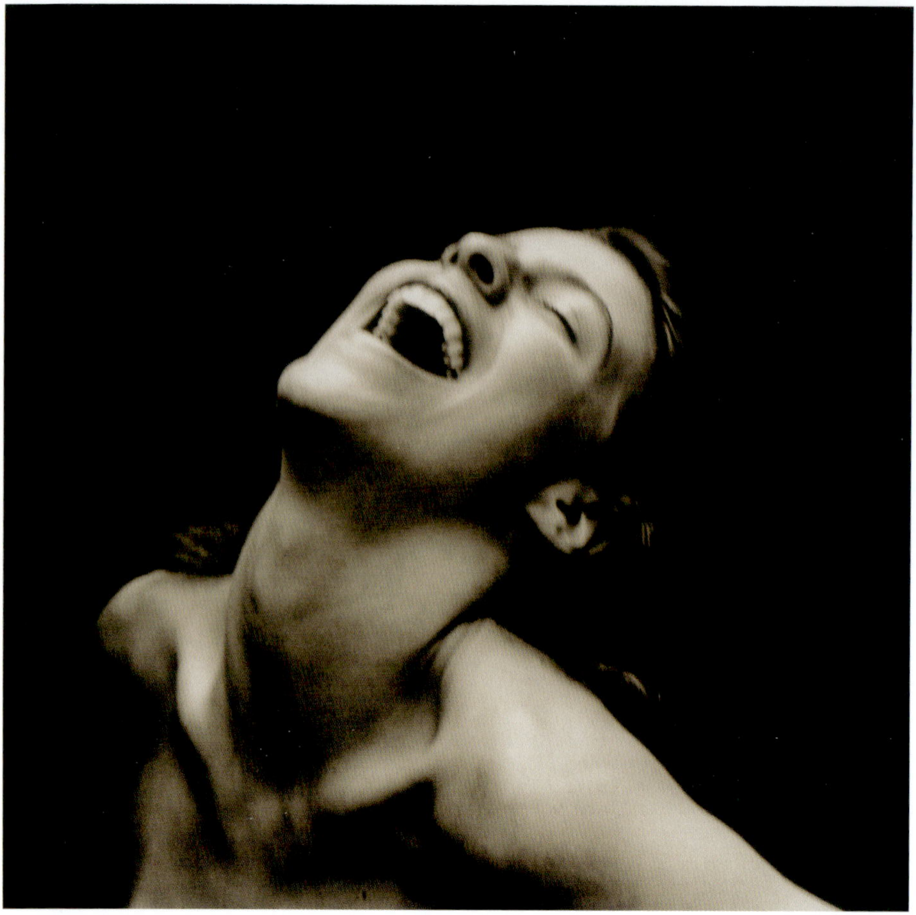

21 LAURA, LONDON, 1989

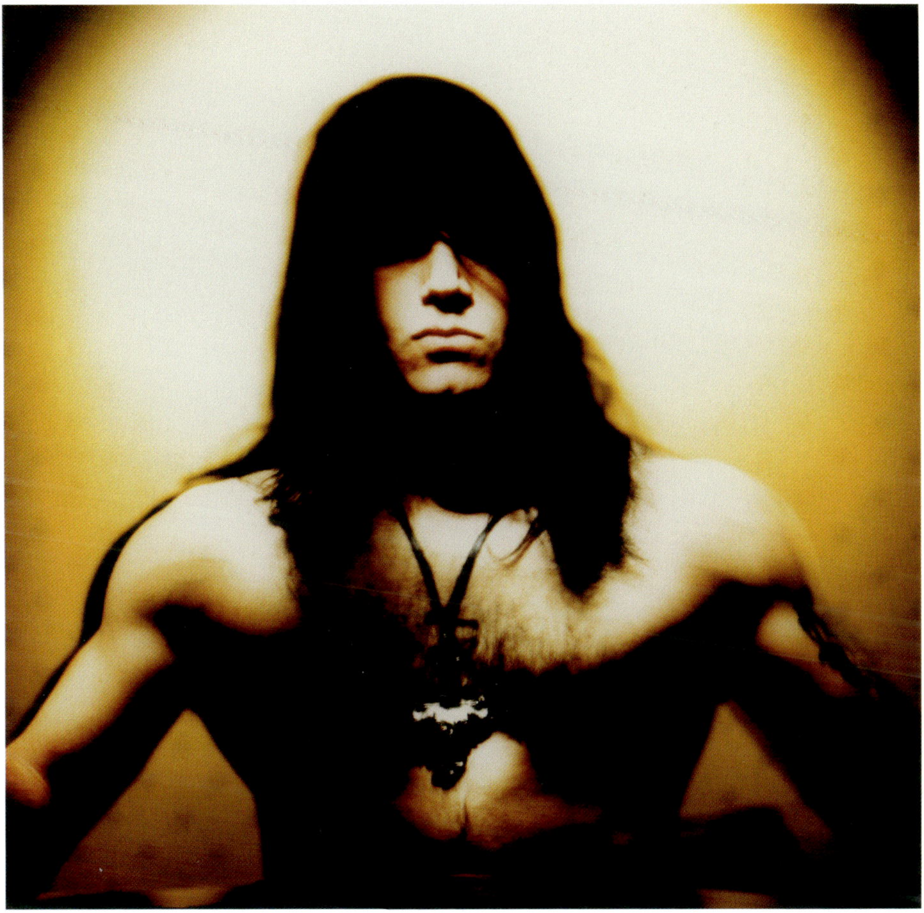

22 GLENN DANZIG, GREEN BAY, 1990

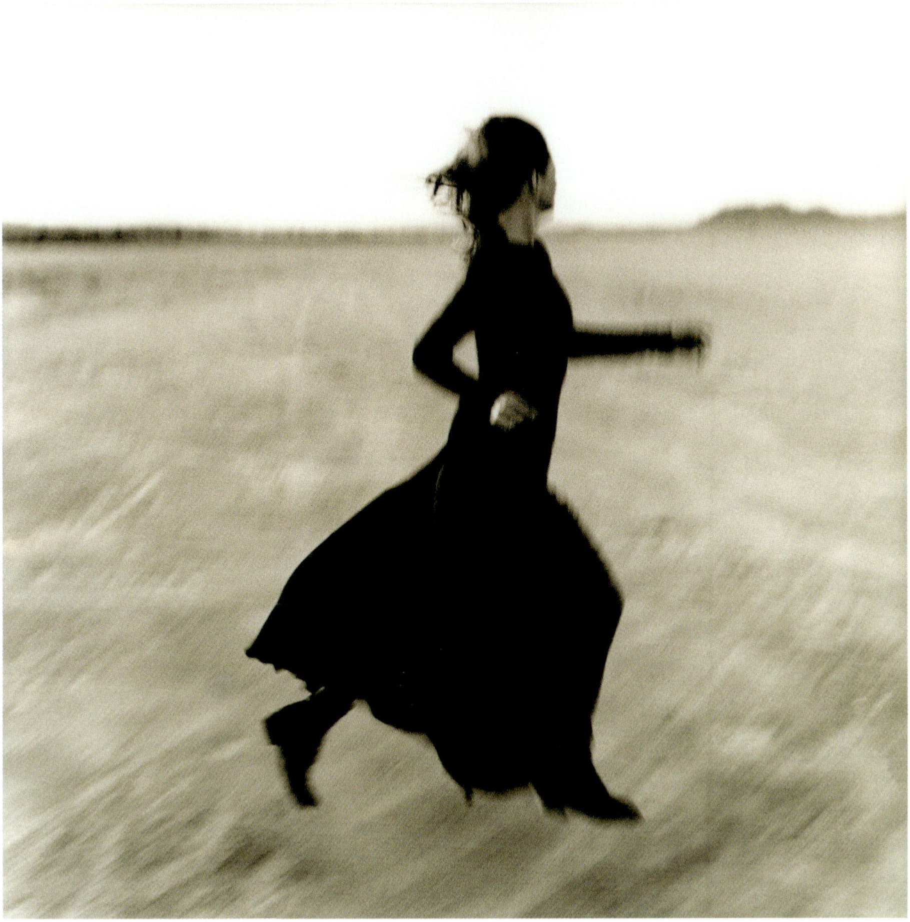

23 SAM PHILLIPS, EL MIRAGE, 1990

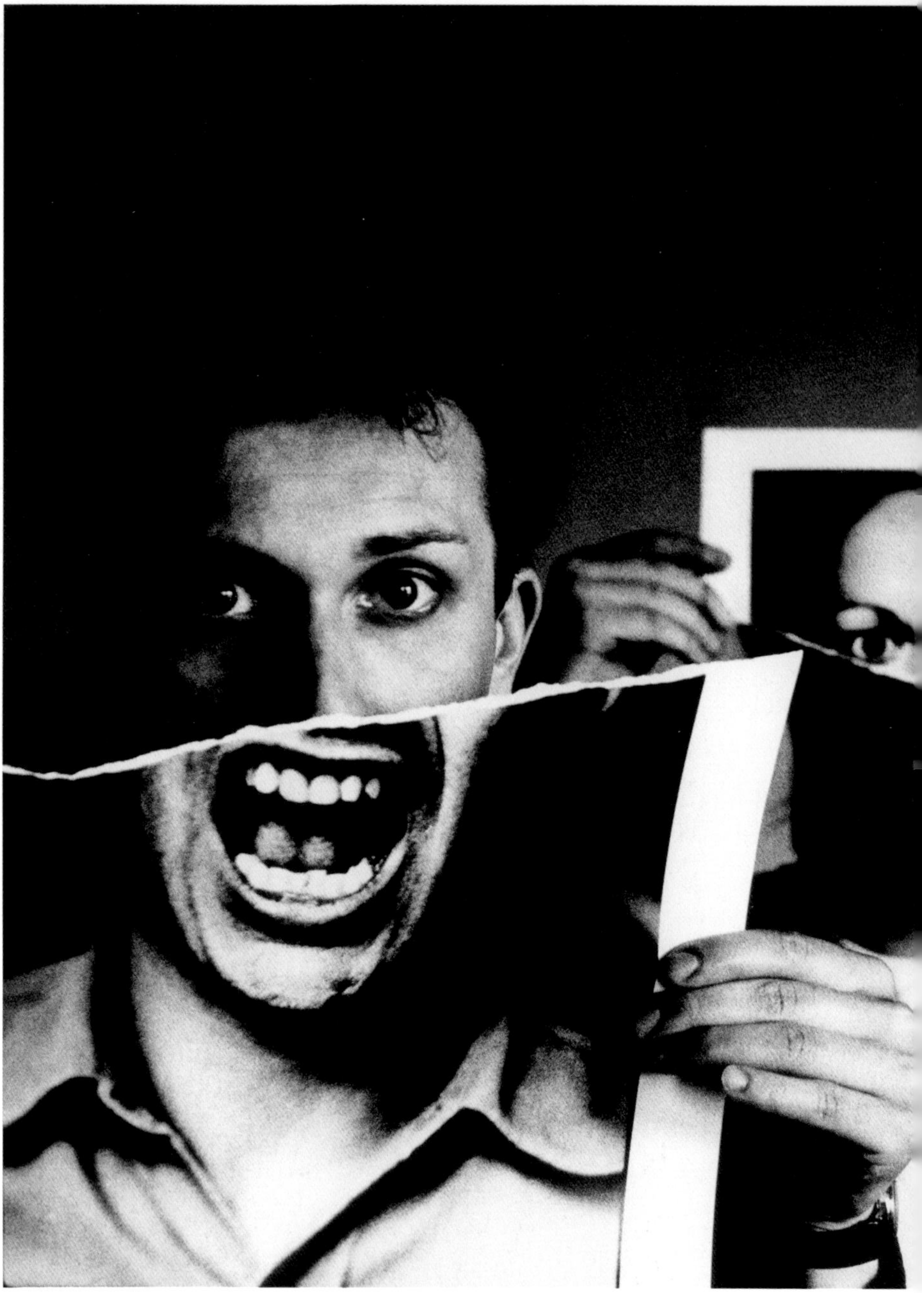

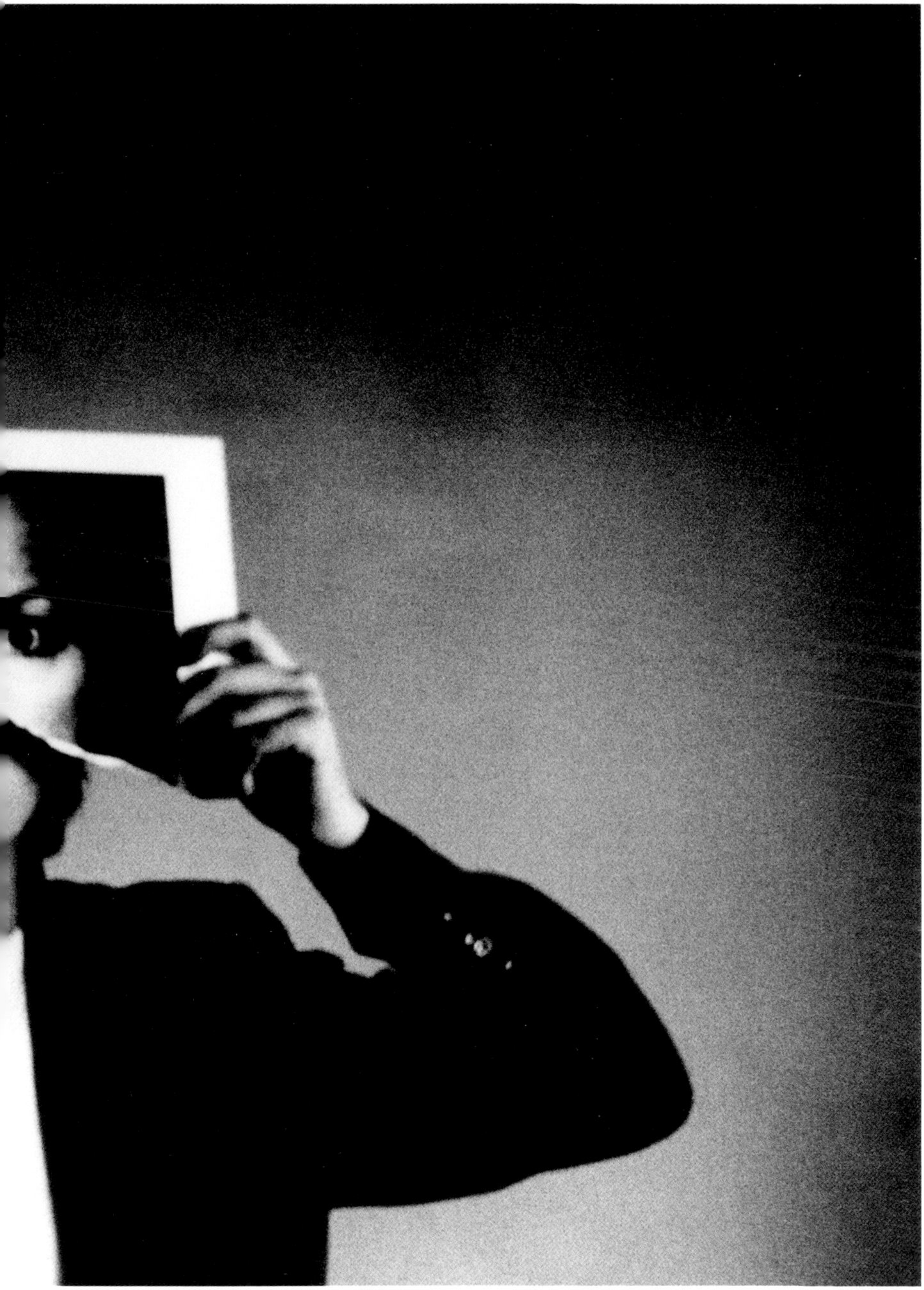

24 CABARET VOLTAIRE, SHEFFIELD, 1983

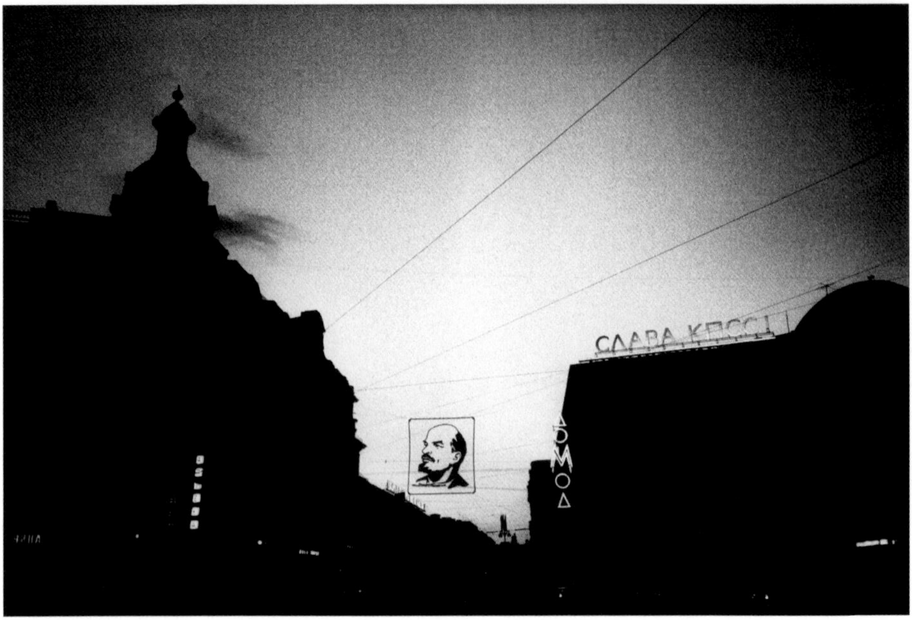

25 PERSON, LENINGRAD, 1983

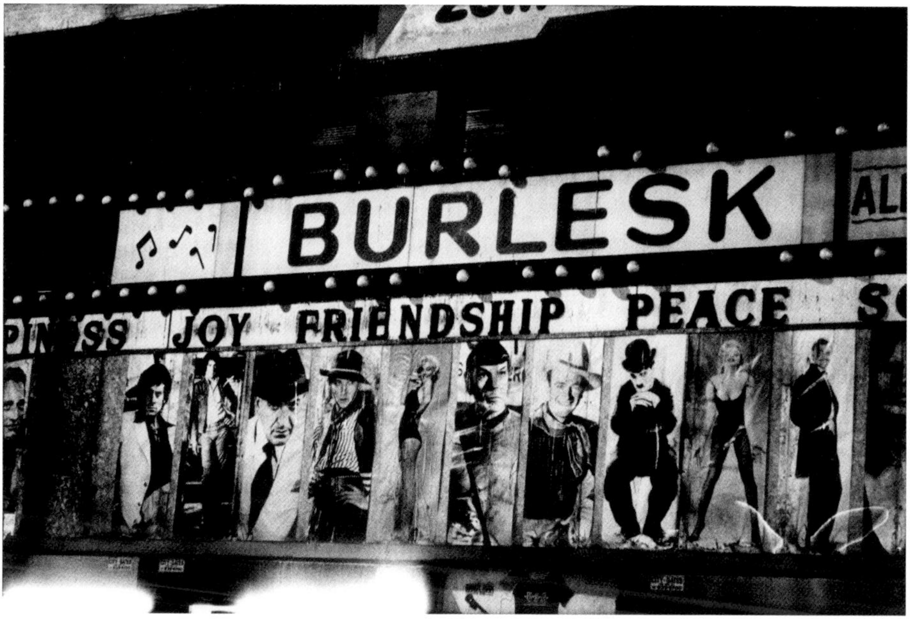

26 PEOPLE, NEW YORK, 1986

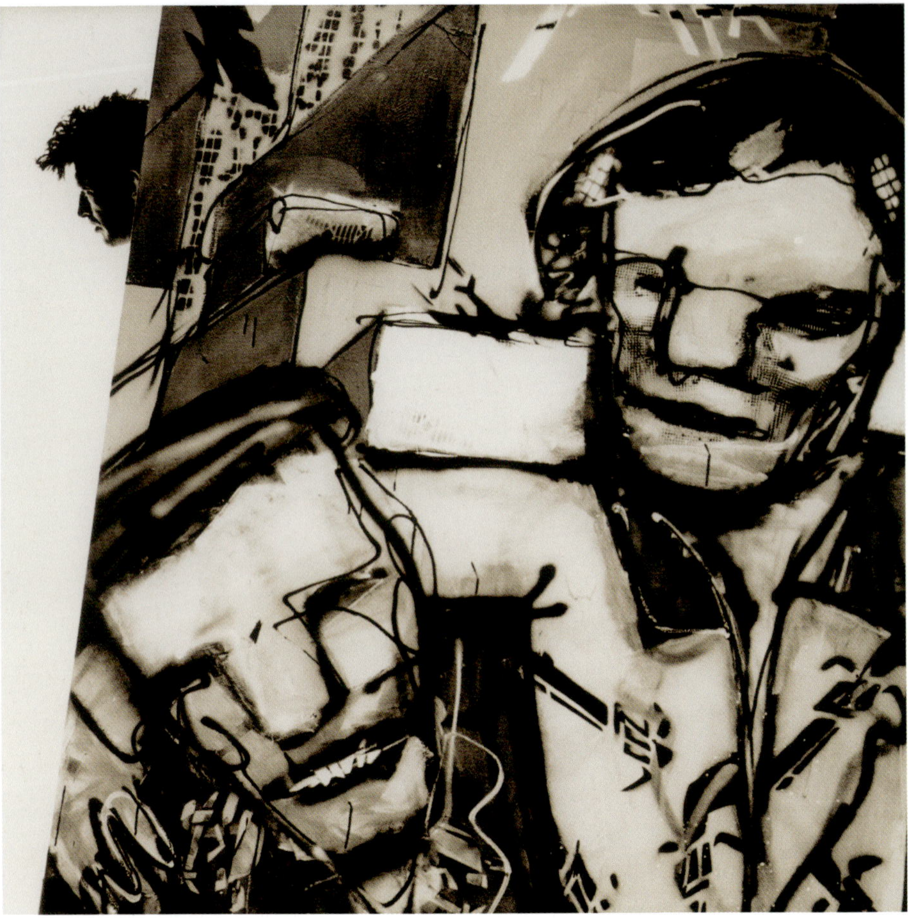

27 HERMANN BROOD, AMSTERDAM, 1989

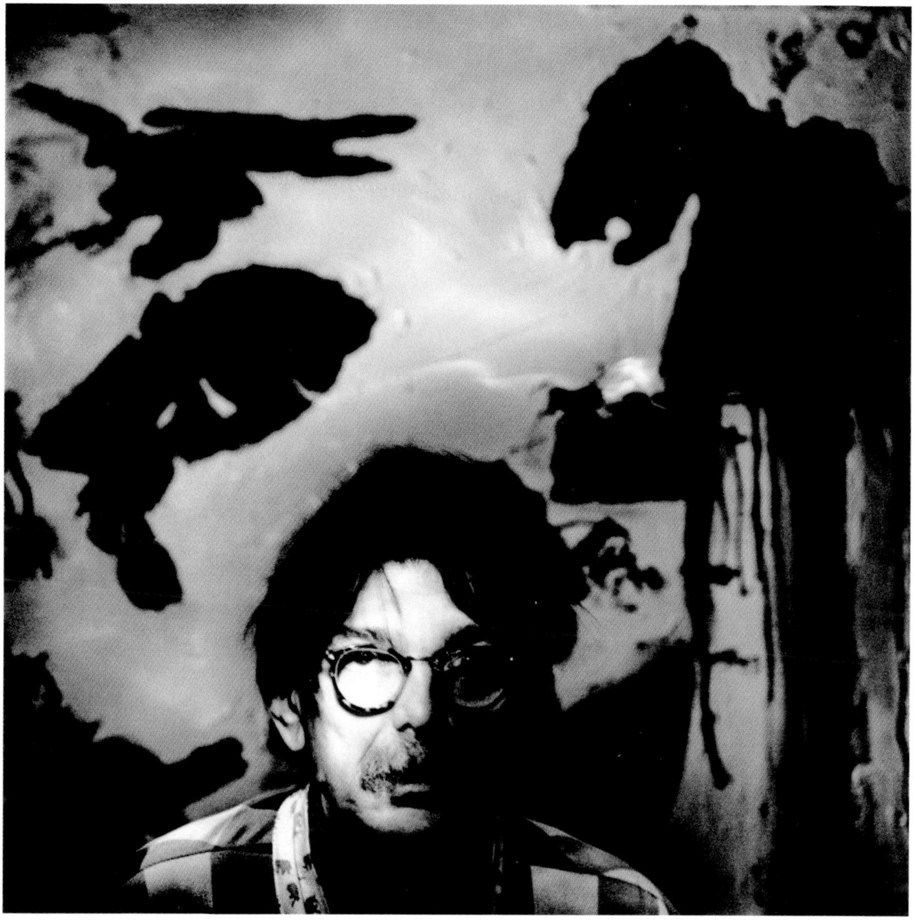

28 DON VAN VLIET, CALIFORNIA, 1990

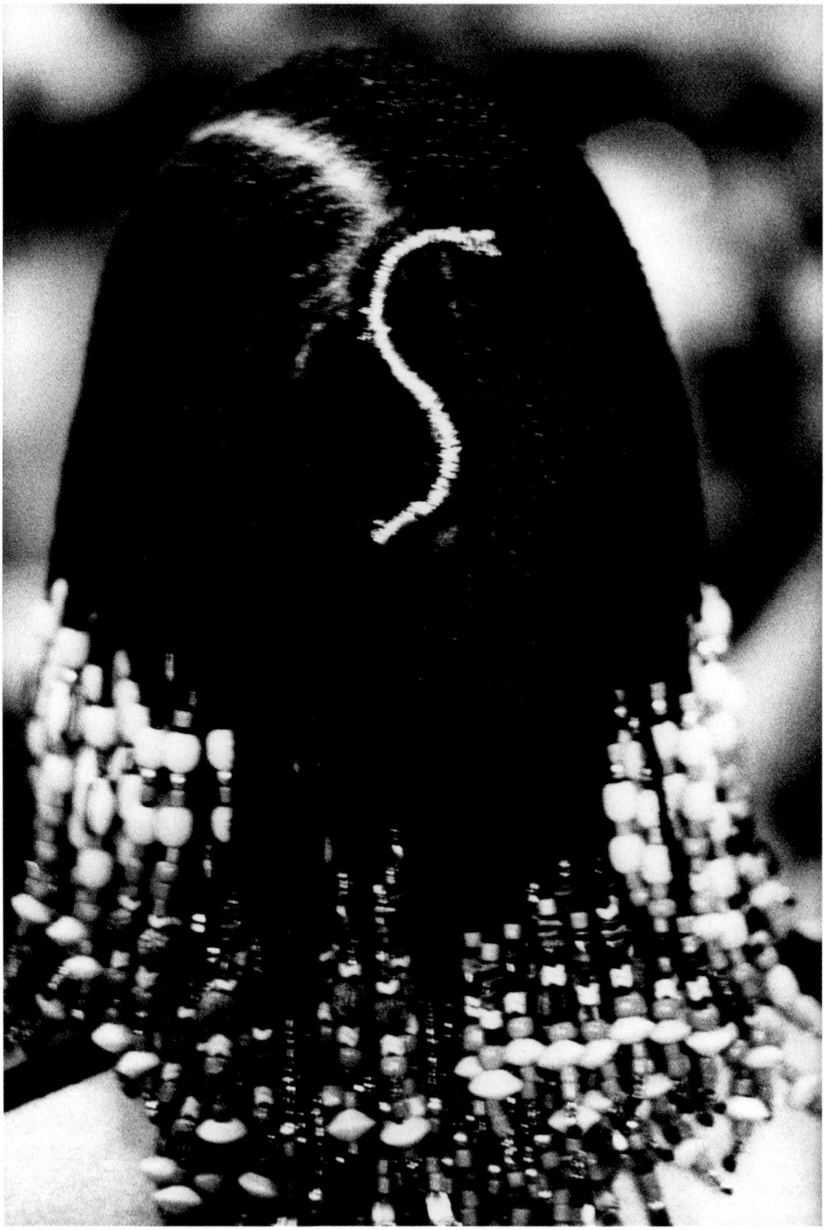

29 STEVIE WONDER, LONDON, 1980

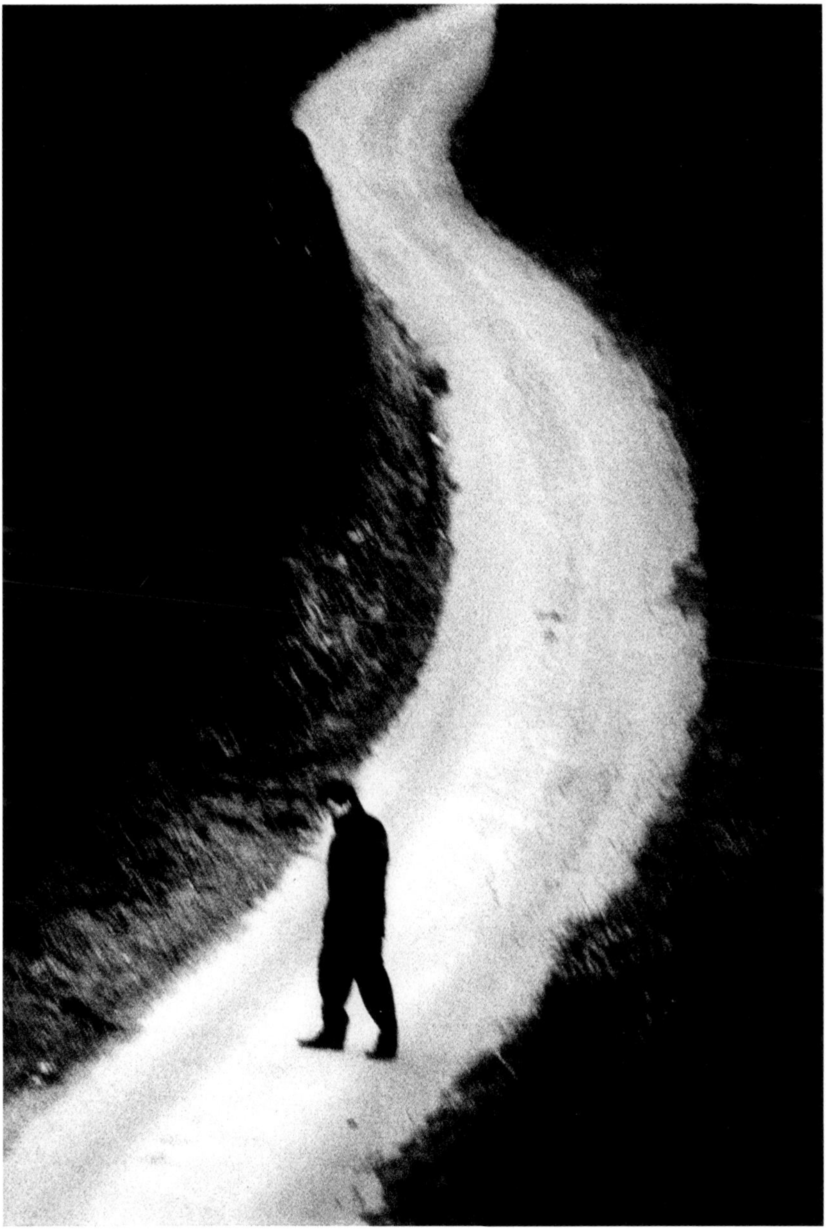

30 PETER GABRIEL, BATH, 1986

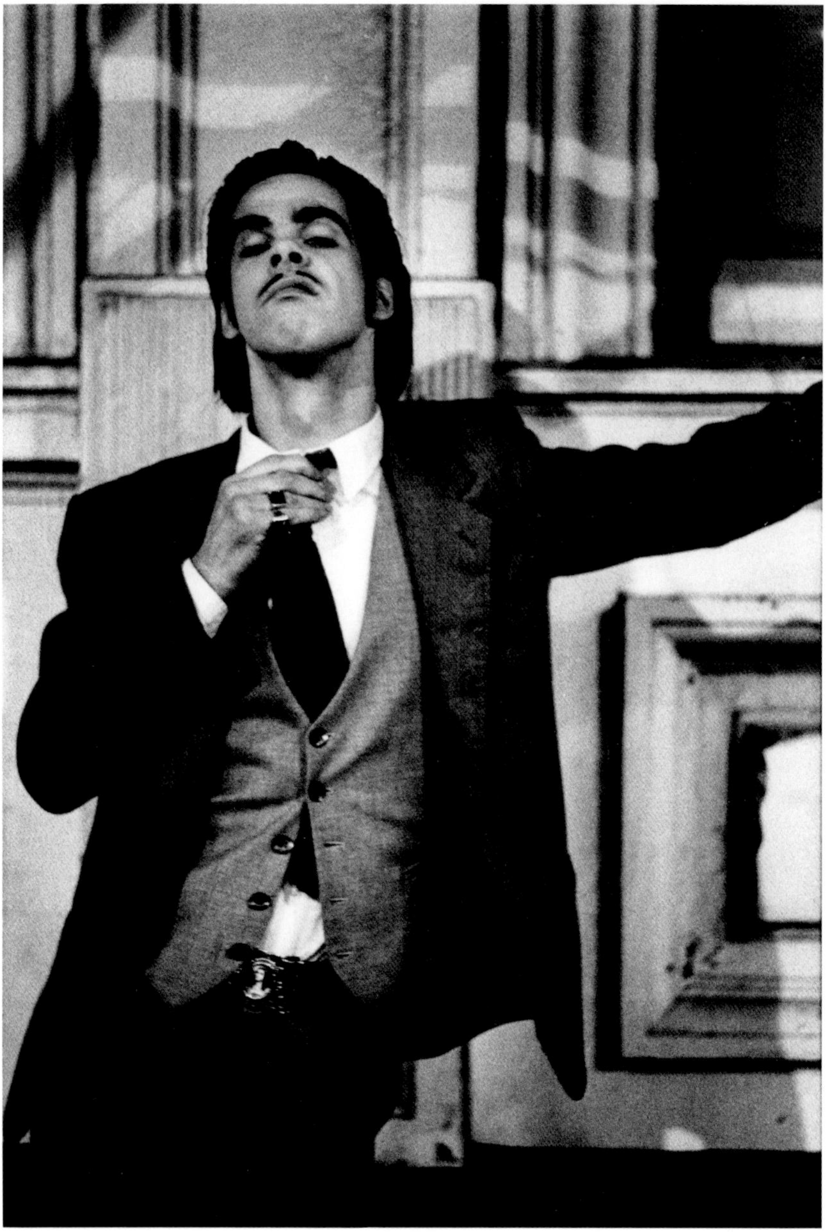

31 NICK CAVE, LONDON, 1988

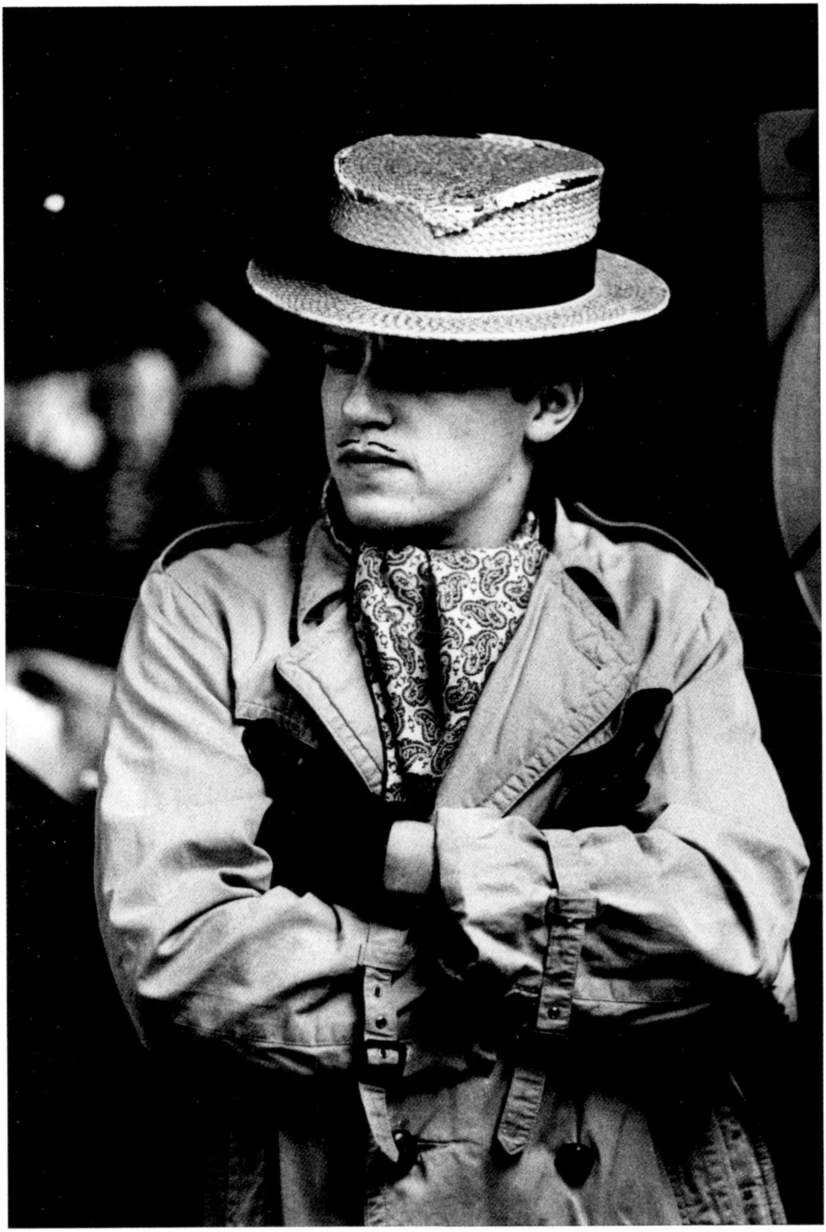

32 SUGGS (MADNESS), BIRMINGHAM, 1980

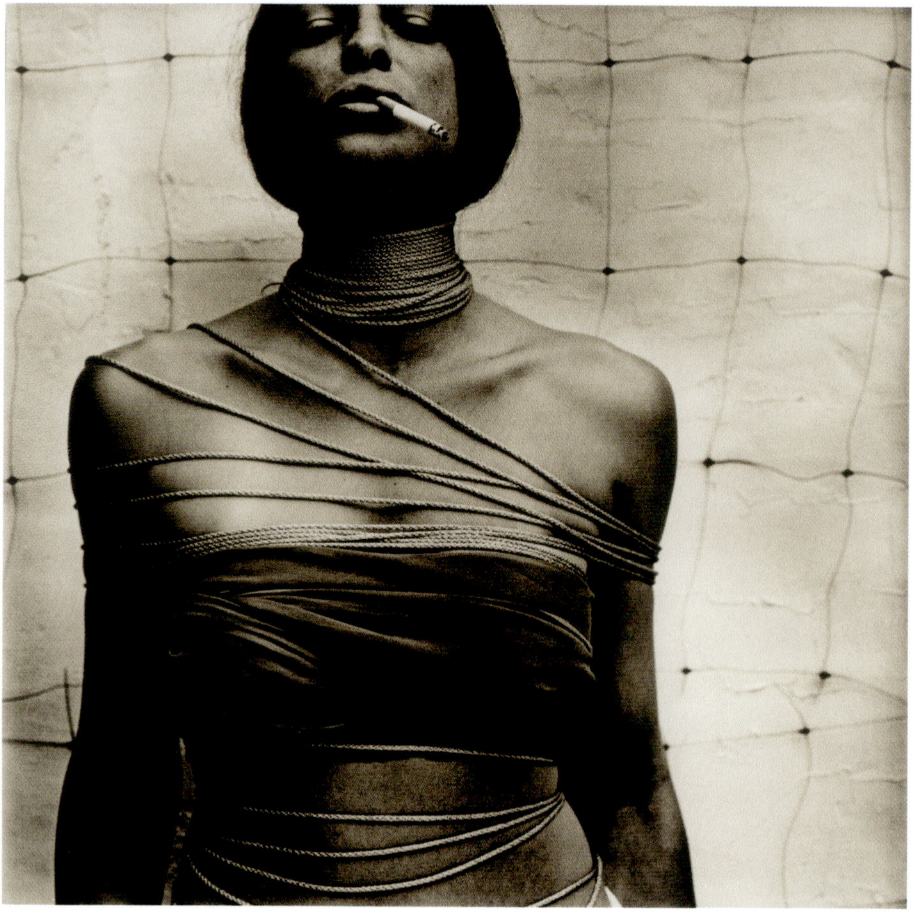

33 LAURA, LONDON, 1989

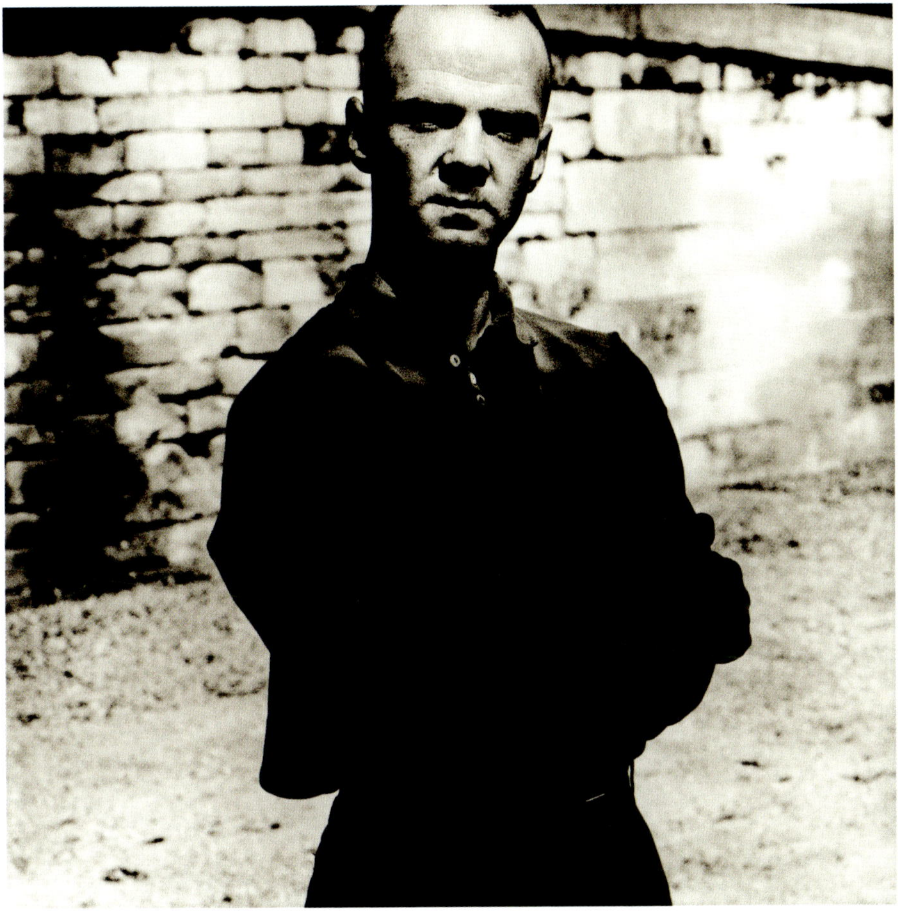

34 JIMMY SOMERVILLE, PARIS, 1989

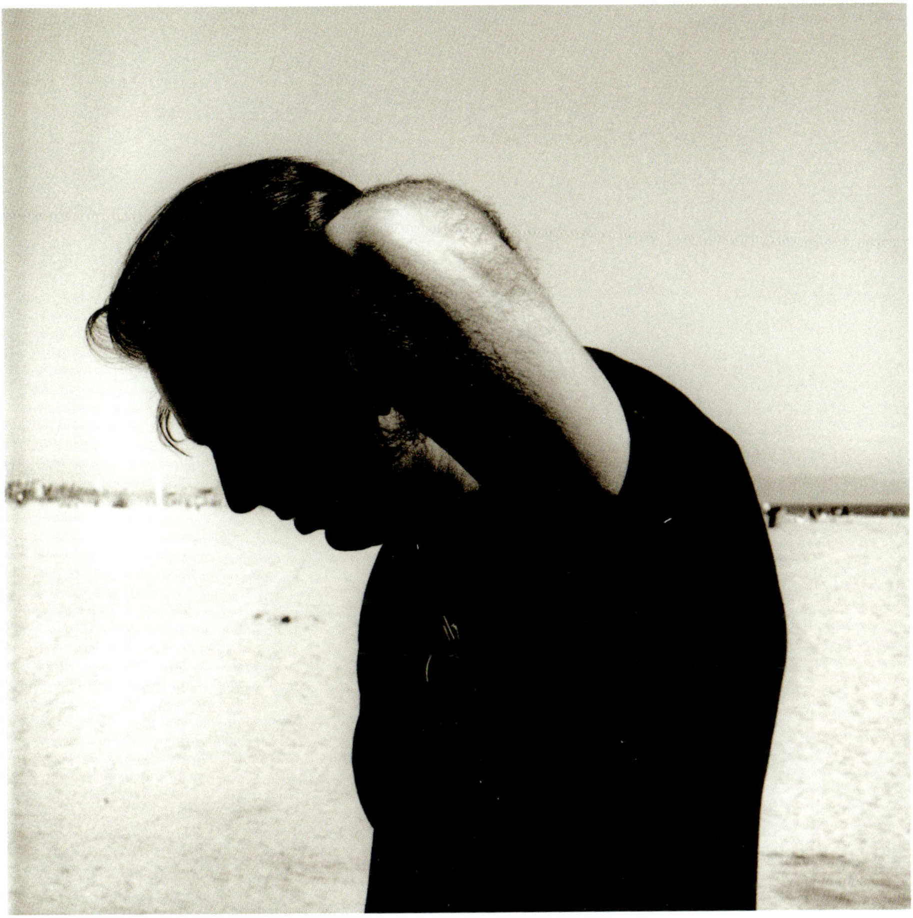

35 NICOLAS CAGE, LOS ANGELES, 1990

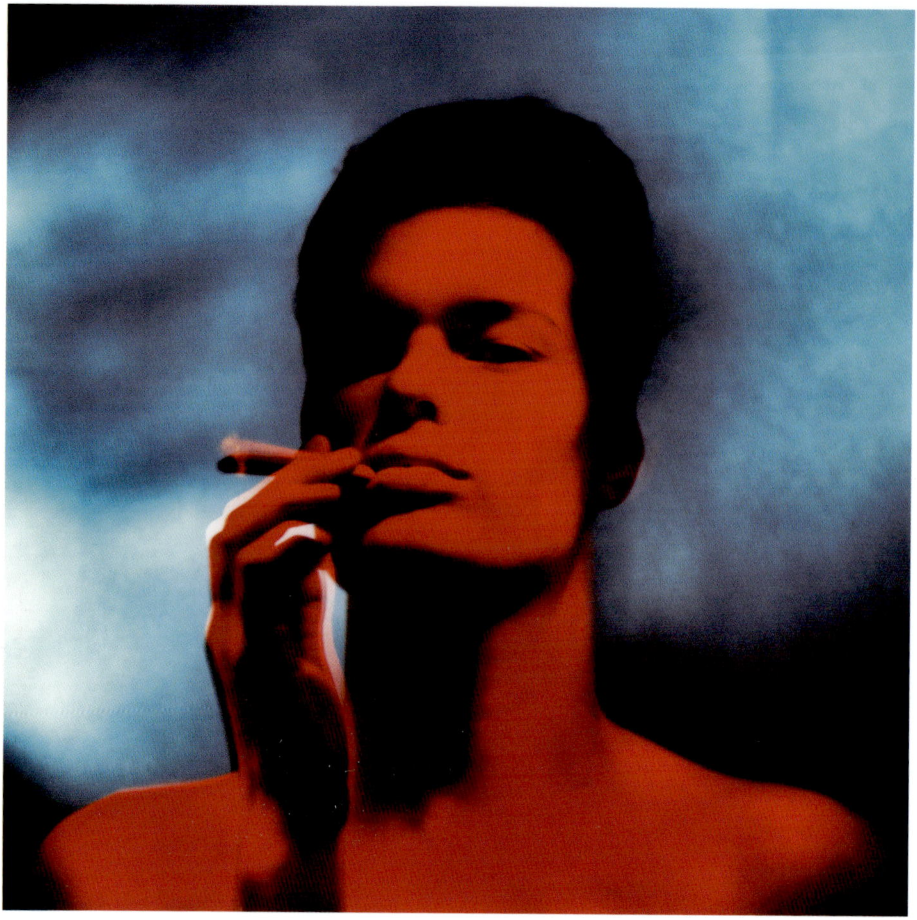

36 BARBARA III, LONDON, 1990

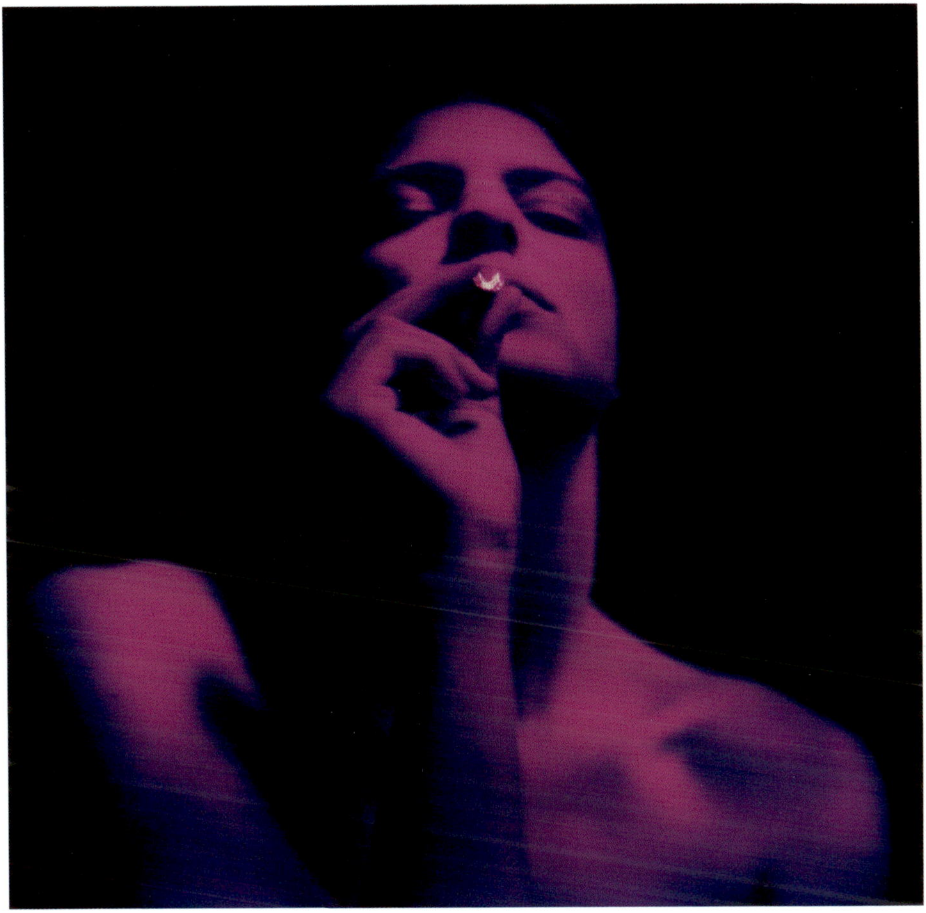

37 LAURA, LONDON, 1989

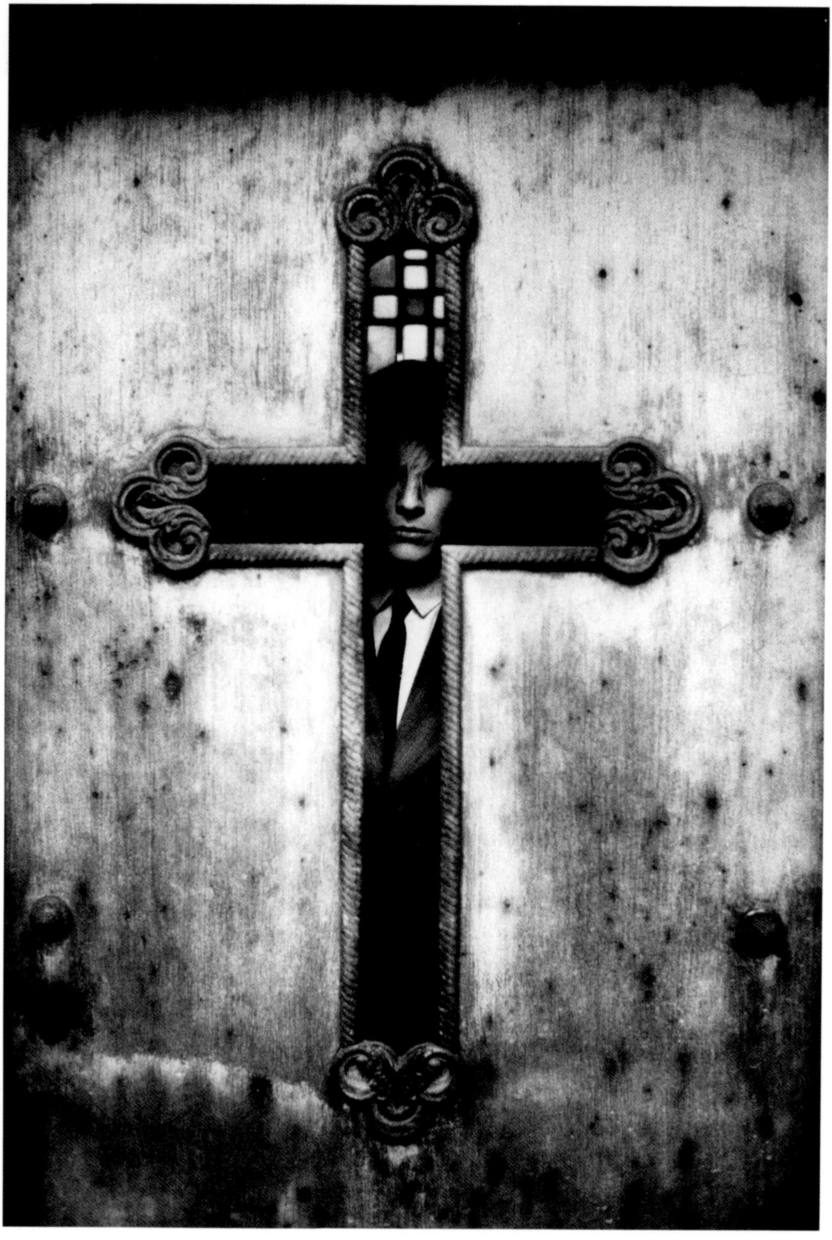

38 DAVID SYLVIAN (JAPAN), PARIS, 1983

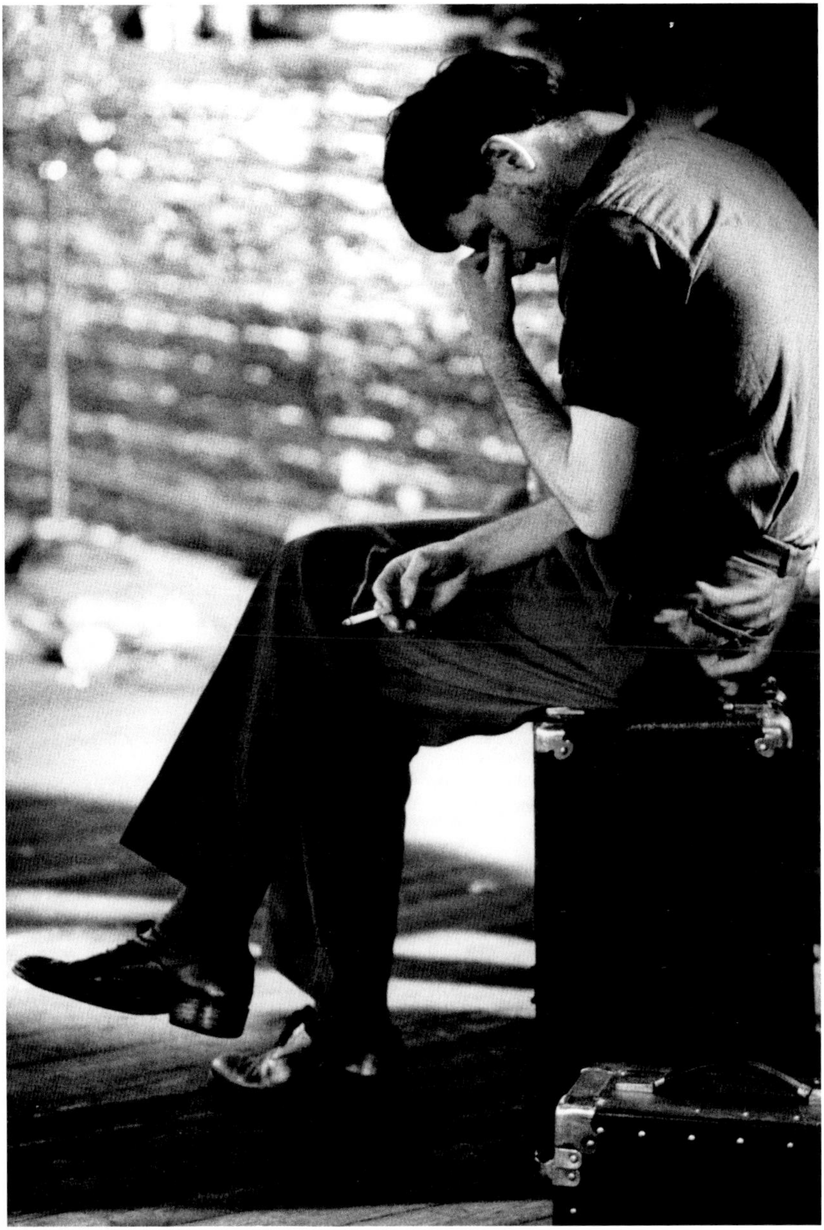

39 IAN CURTIS (JOY DIVISION), MANCHESTER, 1980

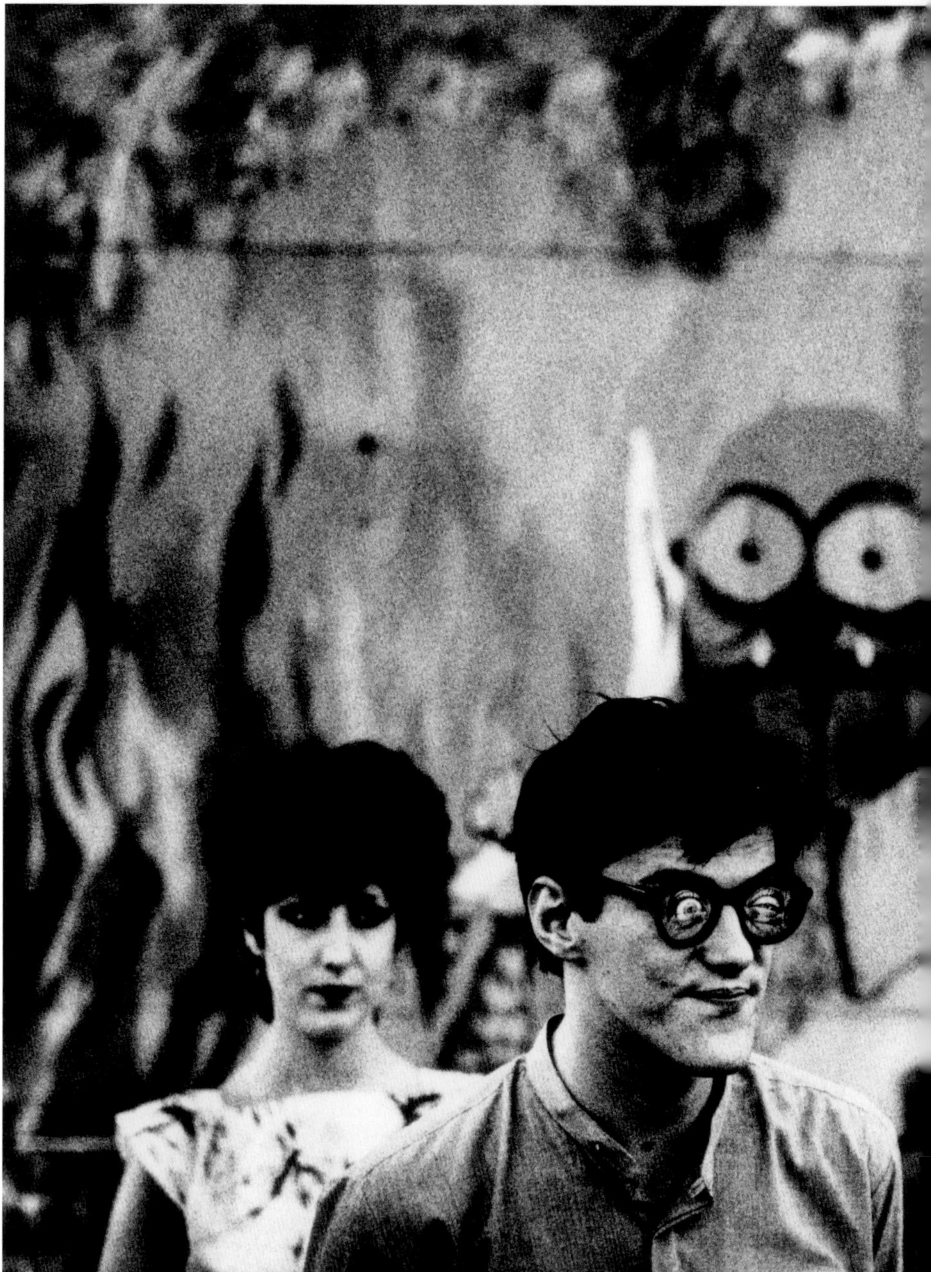

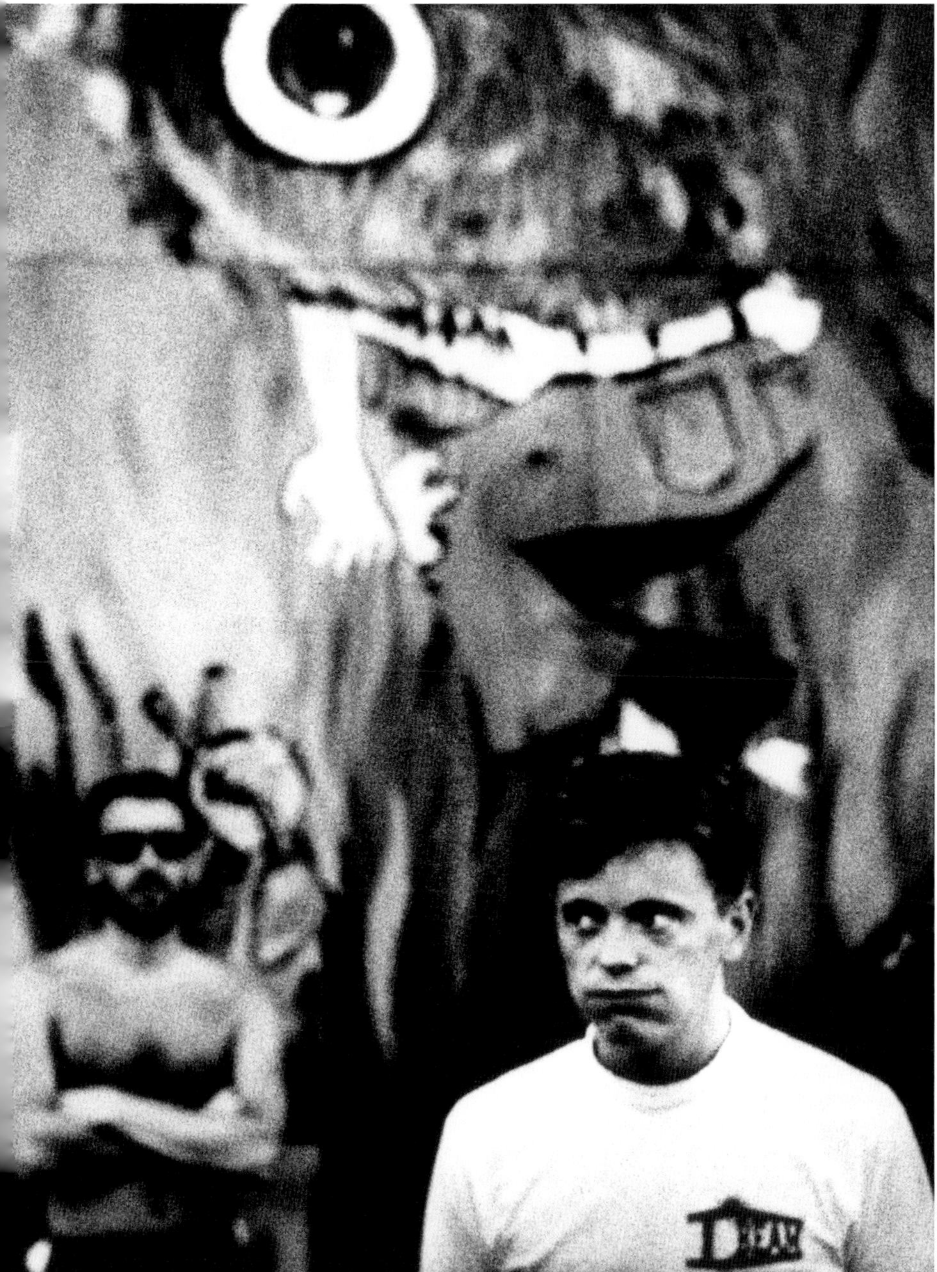

40 NEW ORDER, NEW JERSEY, 1983

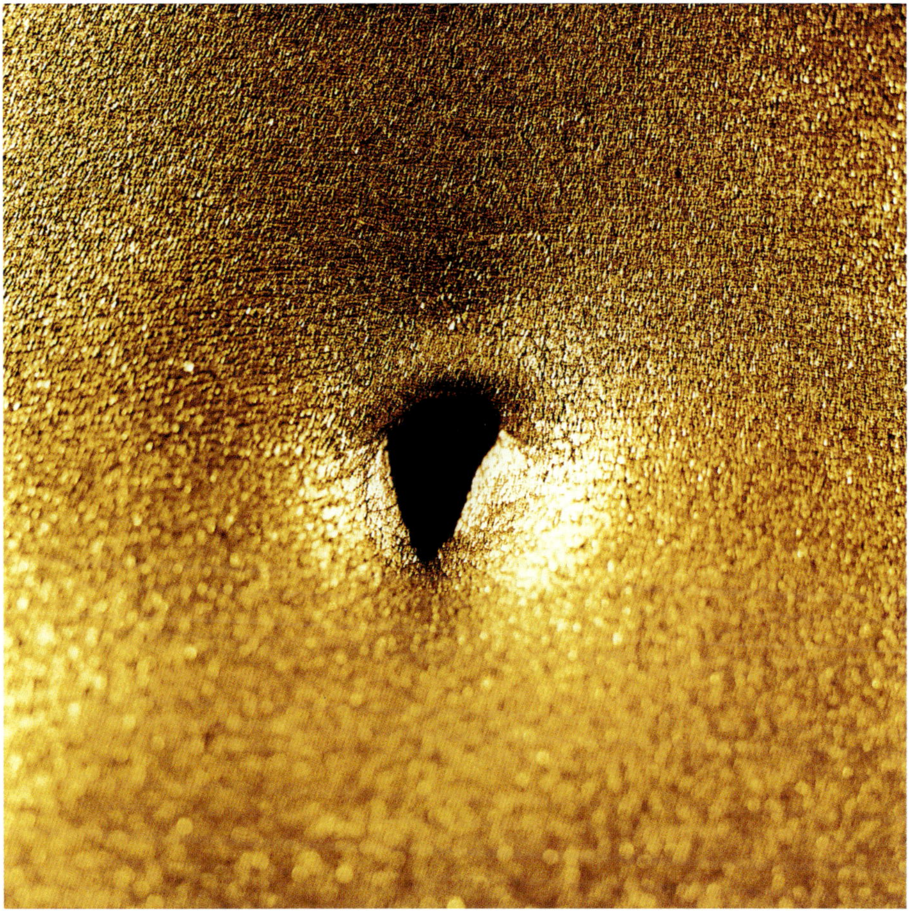

41 GOLDMINE, LONDON, 1990

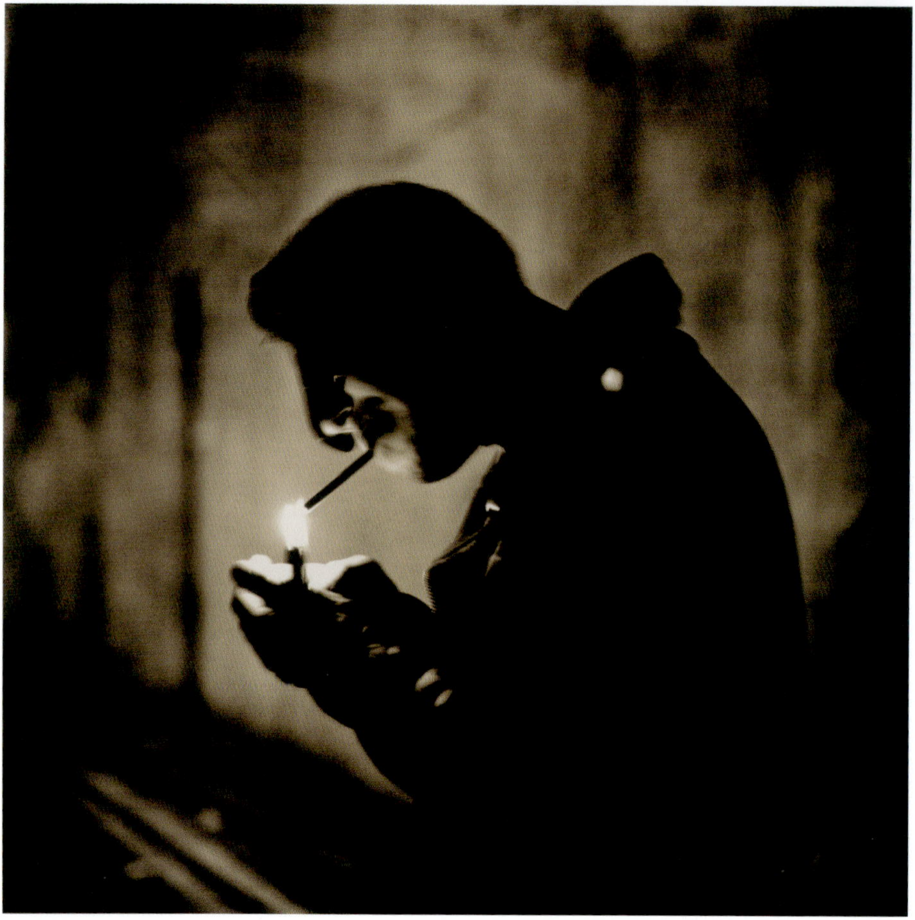

42 ADAM (U2), LONDON, 1988

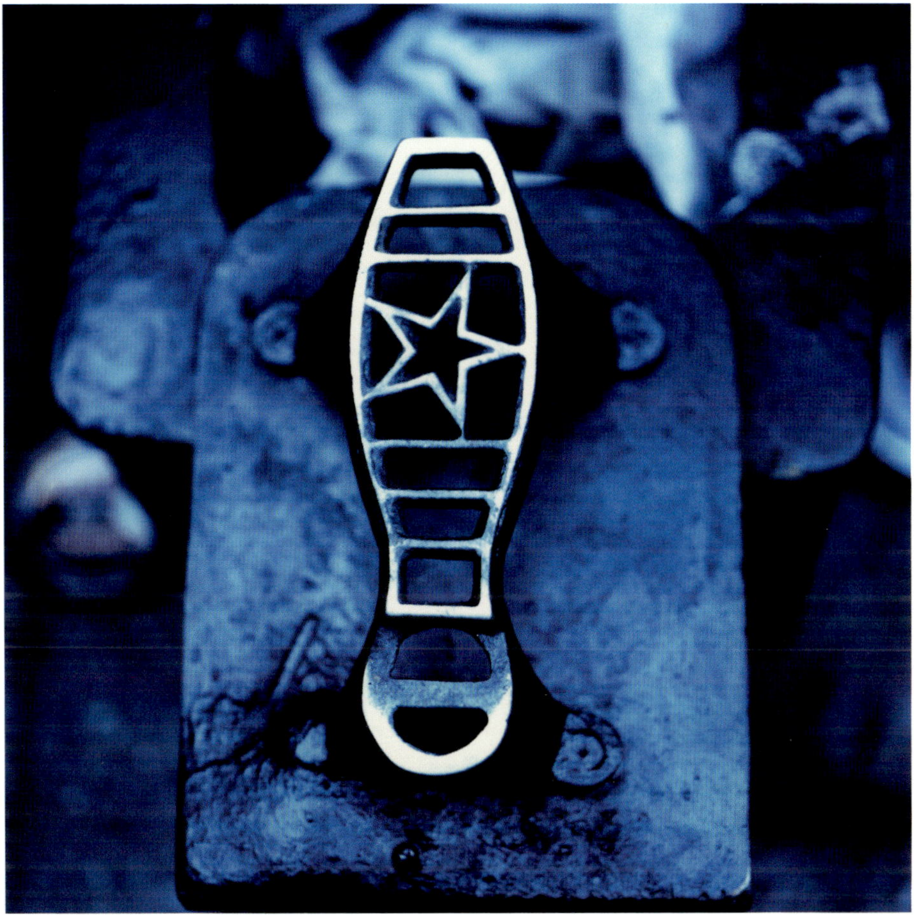

43 STAR, NEW YORK, 1988

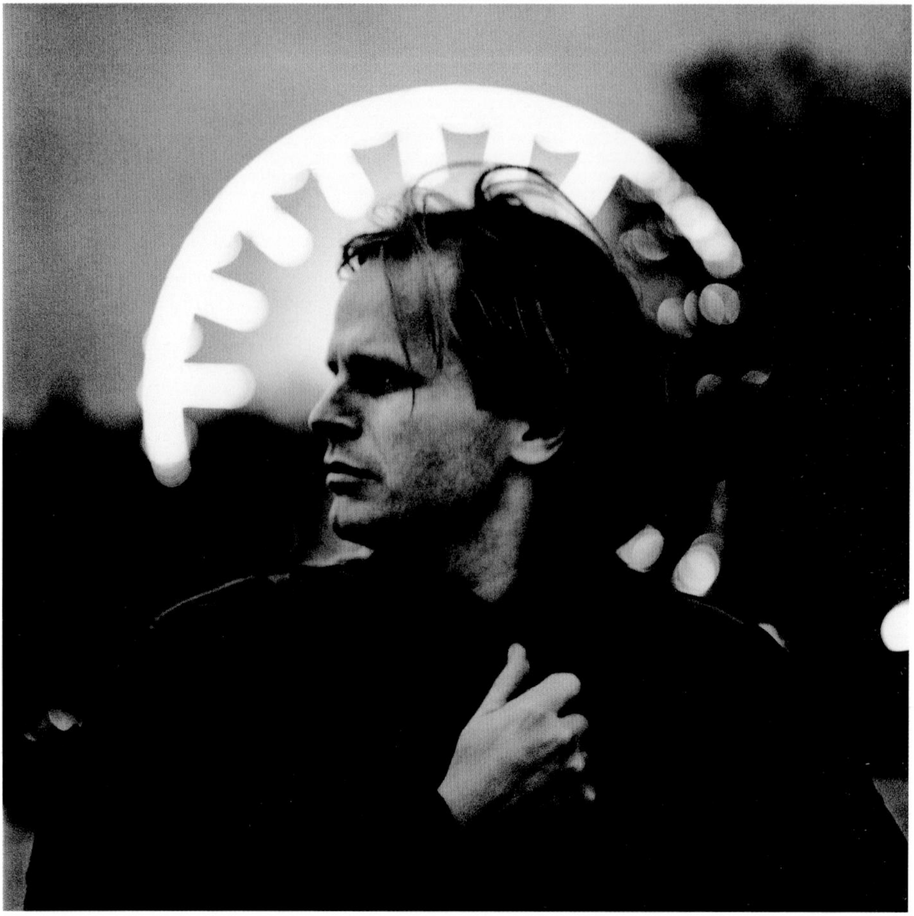

44 HERBERT GRÖNEMEYER, PARIS, 1989

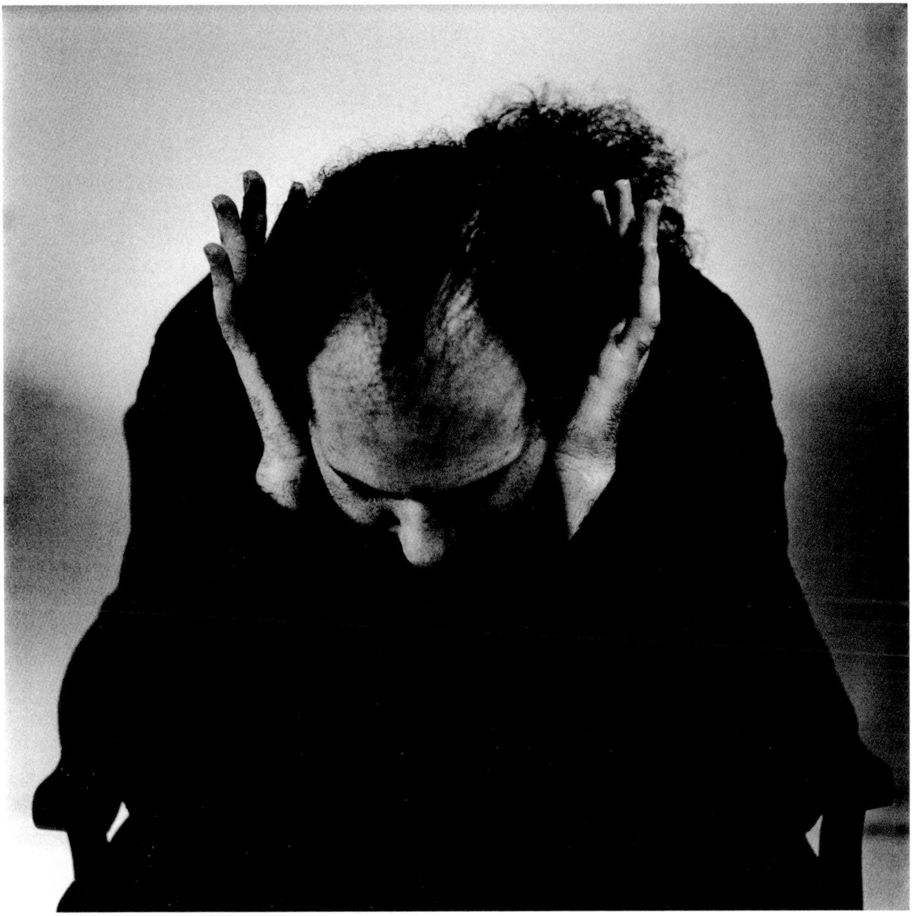

45 HAL WILNER, LONDON, 1989

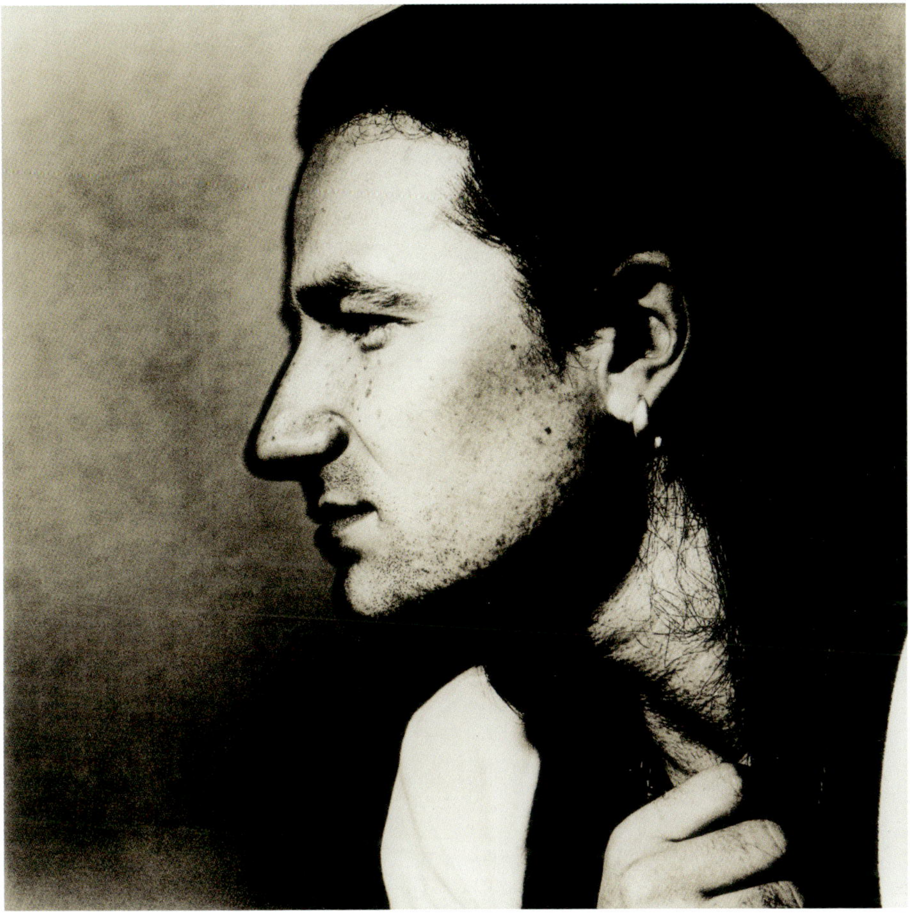

46 BONO (U2), LOS ANGELES, 1988

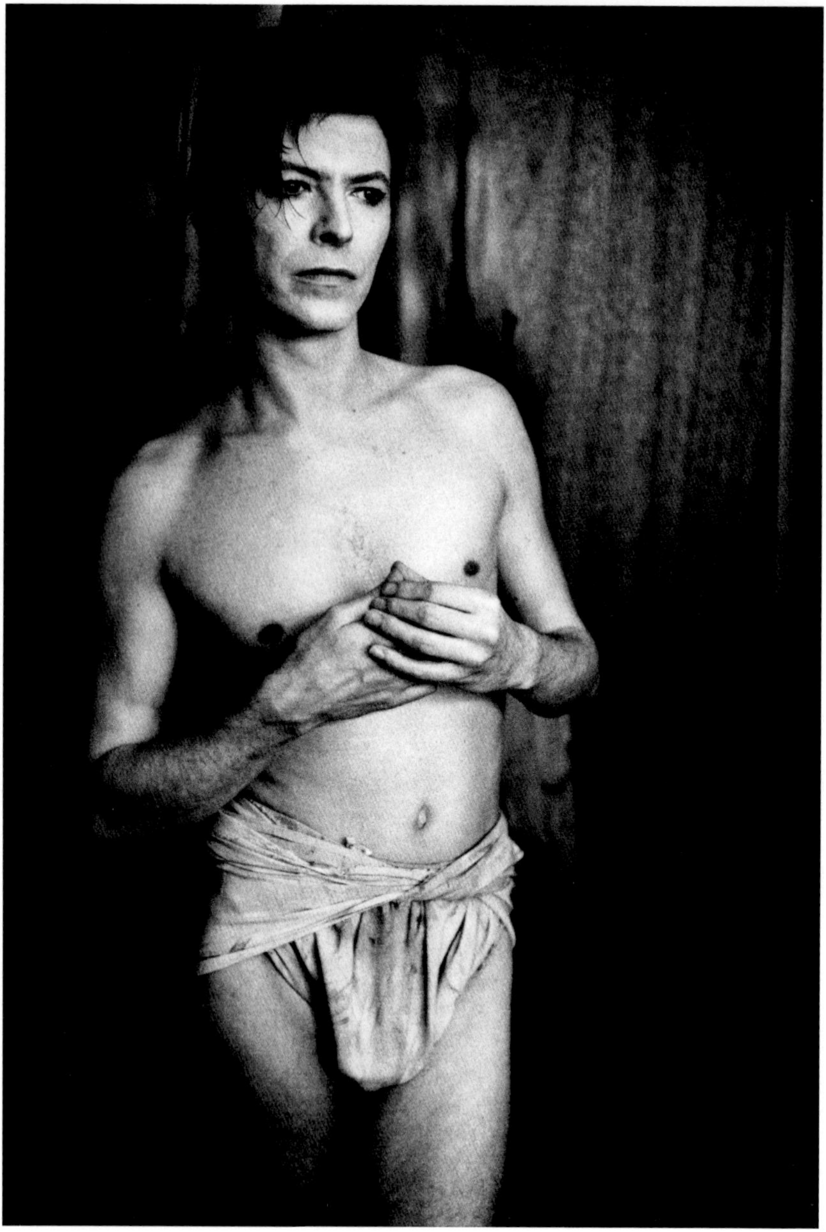

47 DAVID BOWIE, CHICAGO, 1980

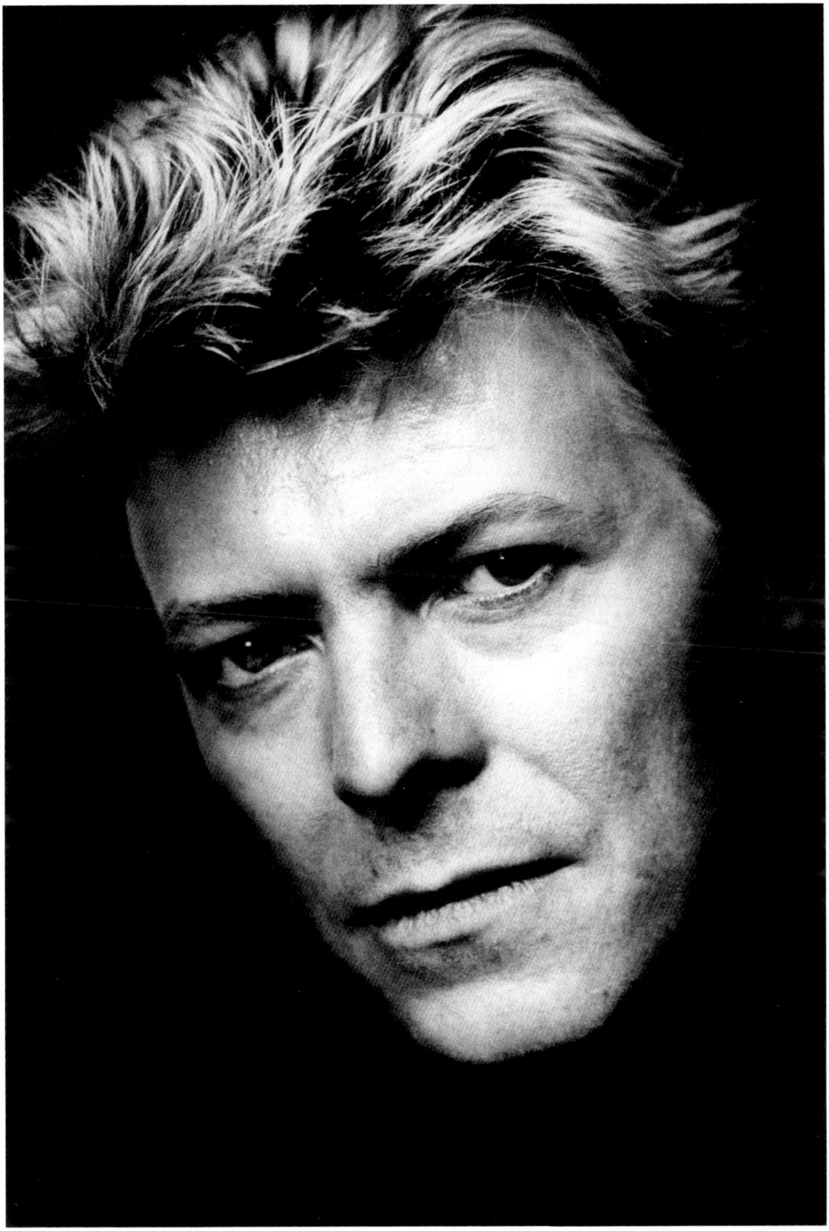

48 DAVID BOWIE, LONDON, 1983

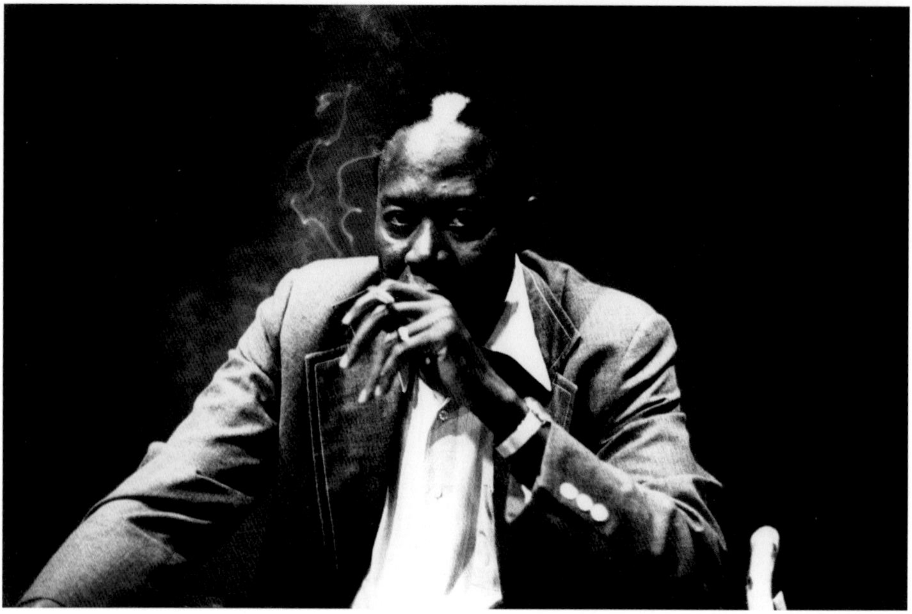

49 MEMPHIS SLIM, GRONINGEN, 1974

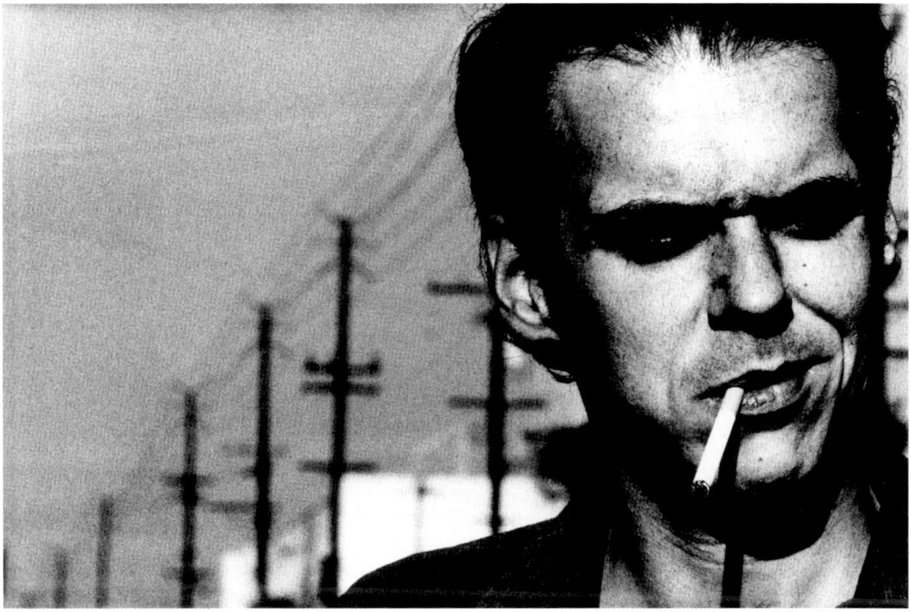

50 JOHN HIATT, LOS ANGELES, 1981

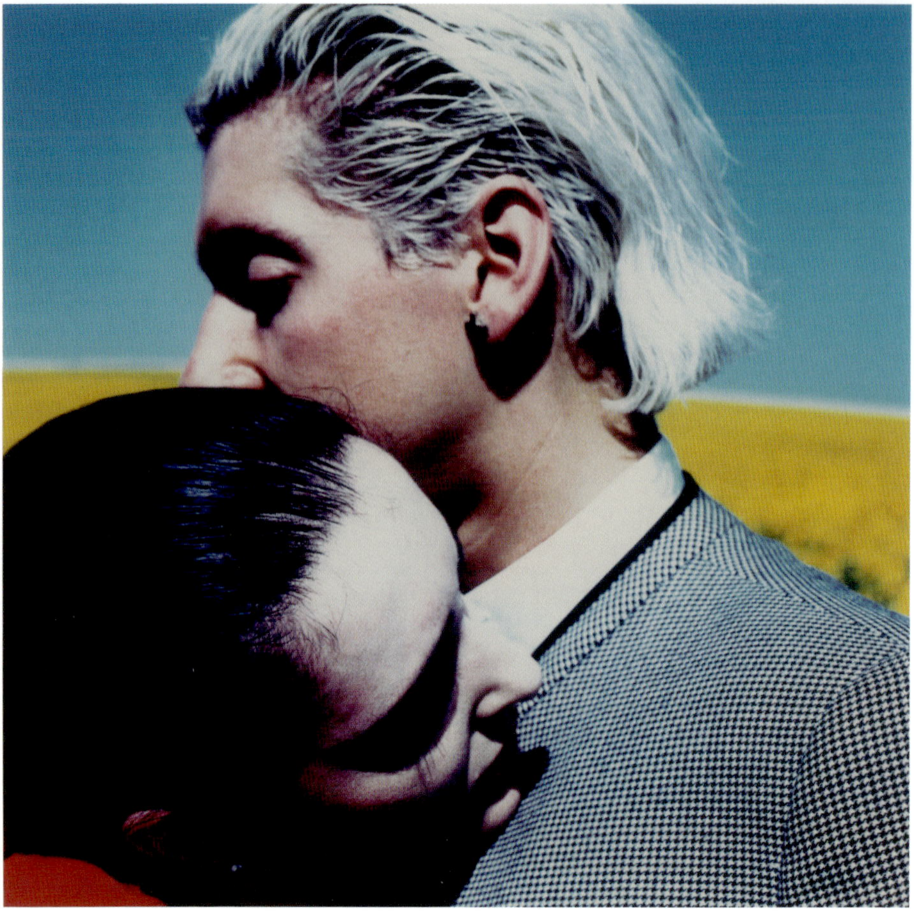

51 THE CREATURES, SEVILLA, 1989

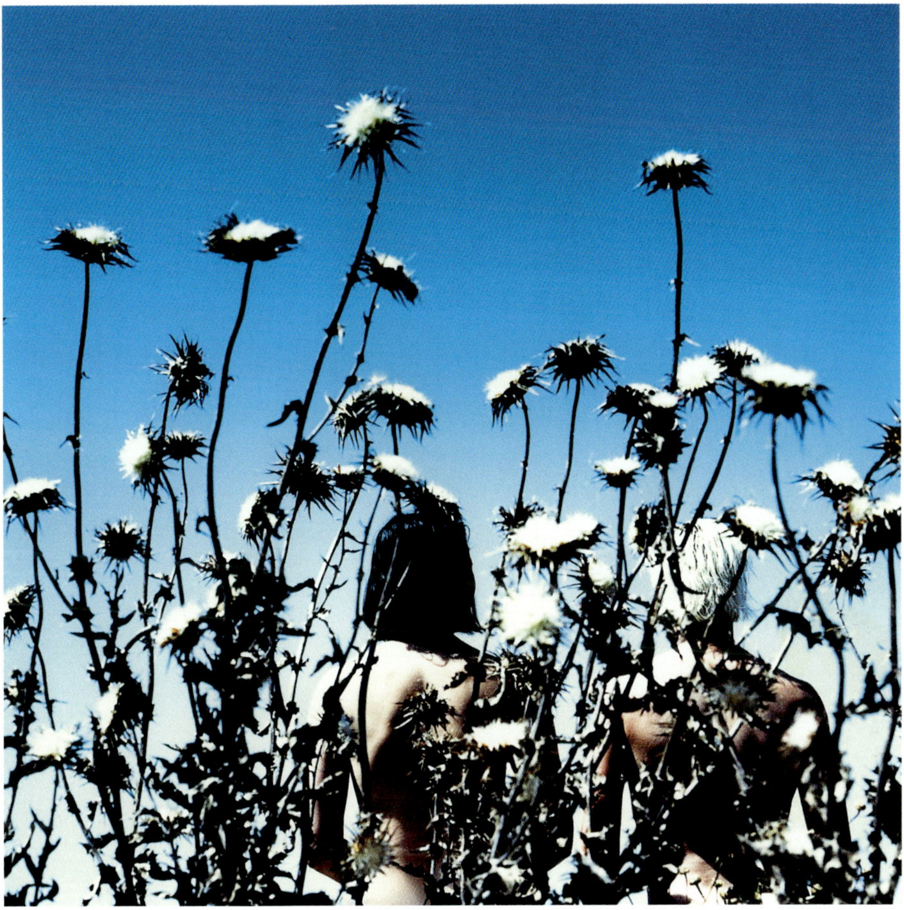

52 THE CREATURES, SEVILLA, 1989

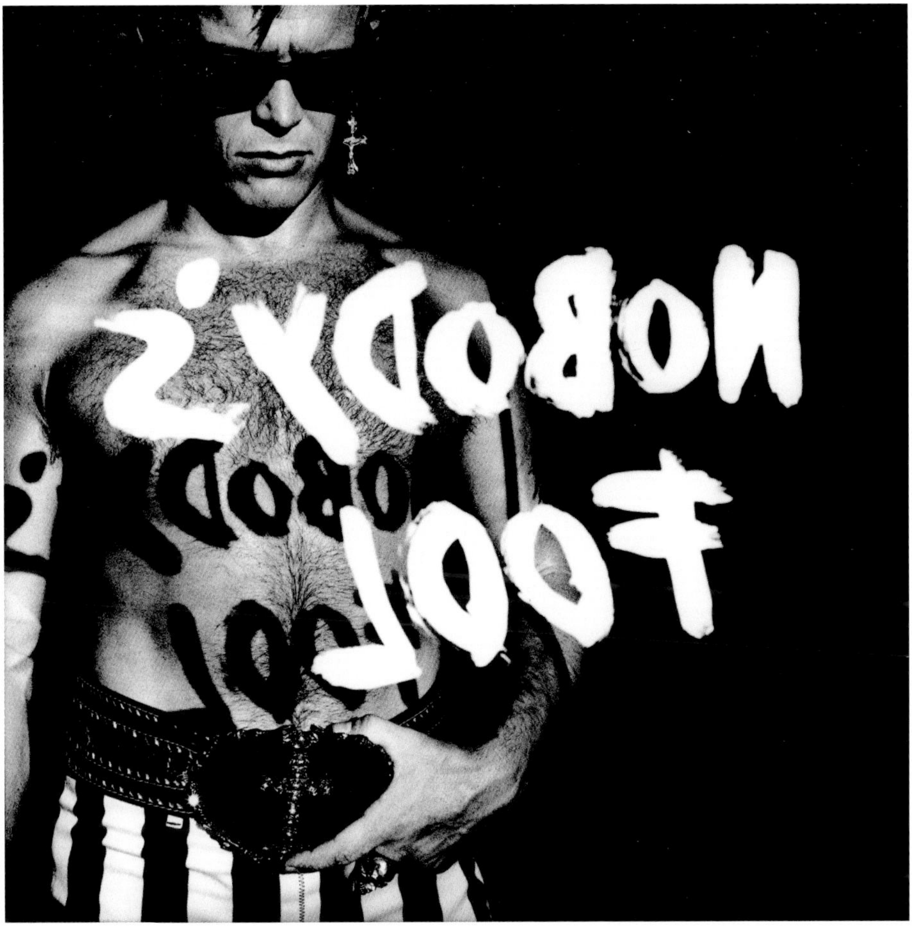

53 BILLY IDOL, LOS ANGELES, 1990

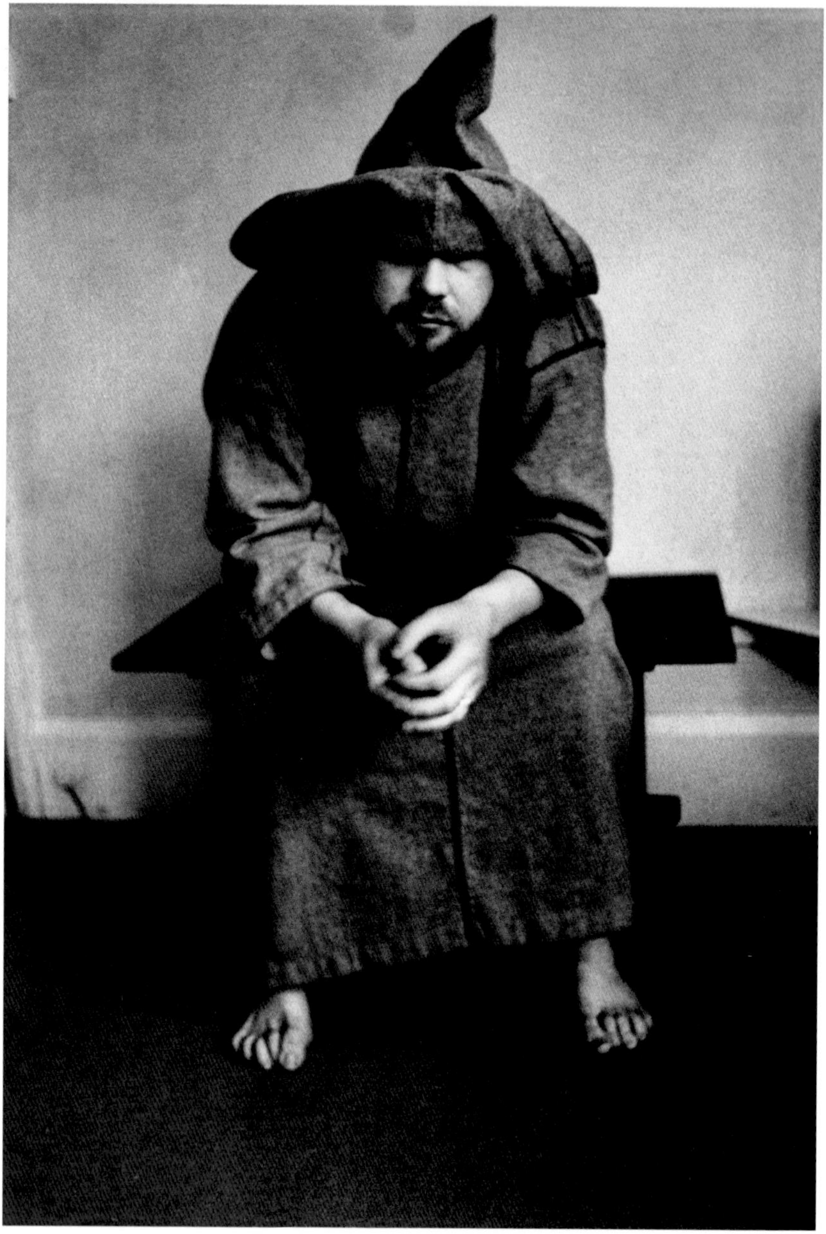

54 JOHN MARTYN, HEATHFIELD, 1978

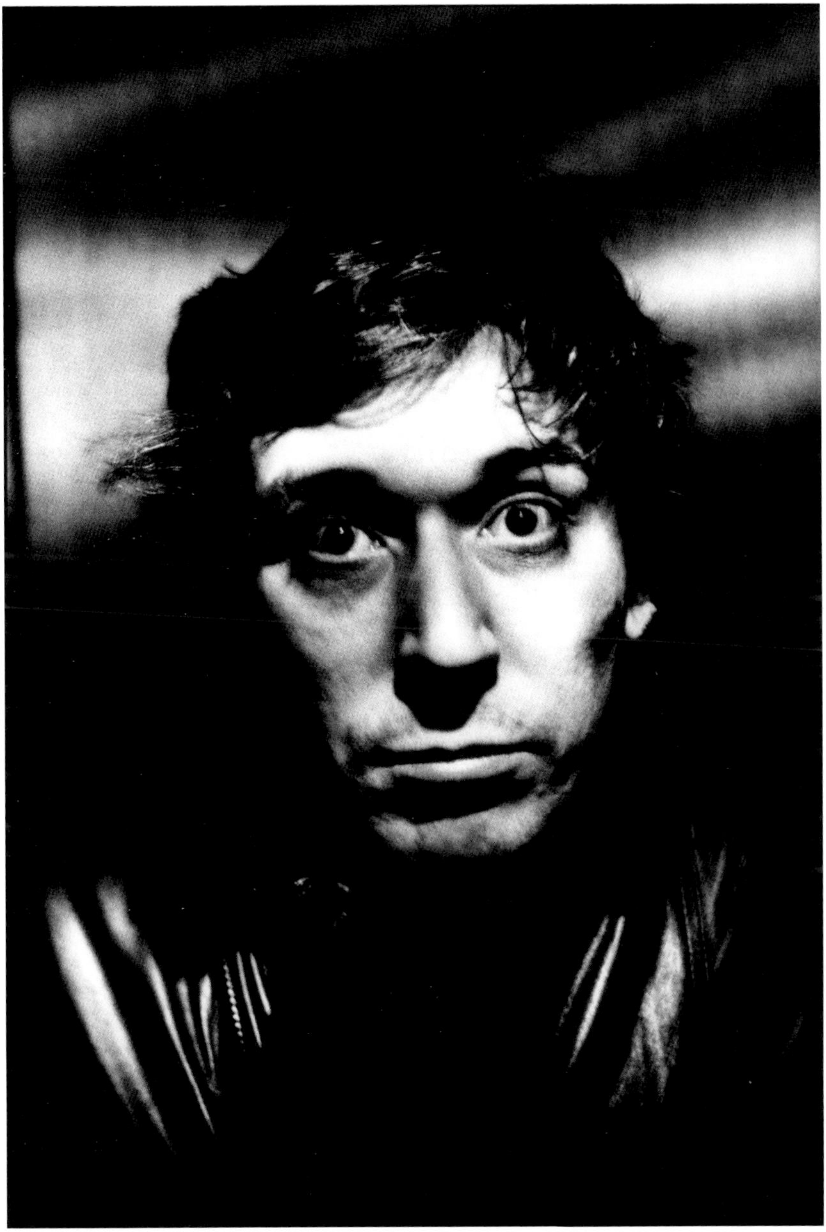

55 JOHN CALE, LONDON, 1983

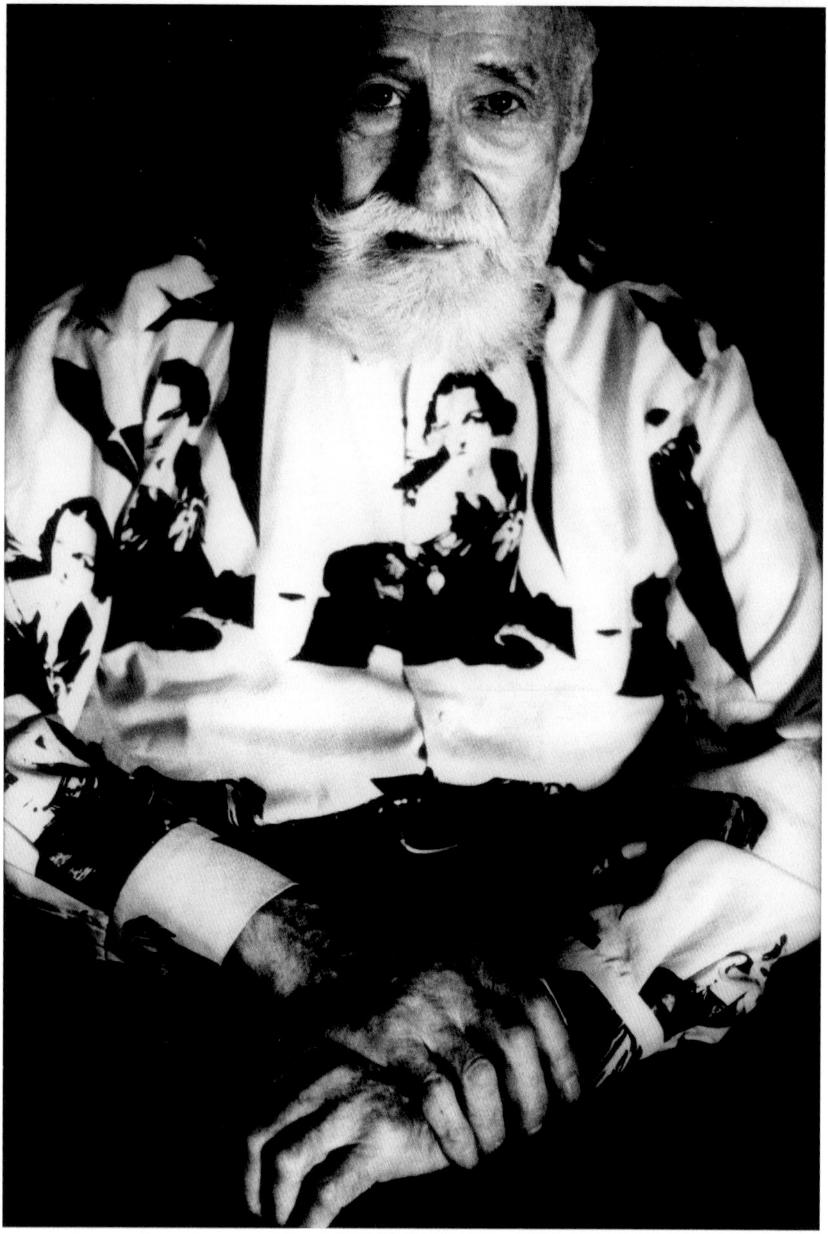

56 ANGUS MCBEAN, DEBENHAM, 1986

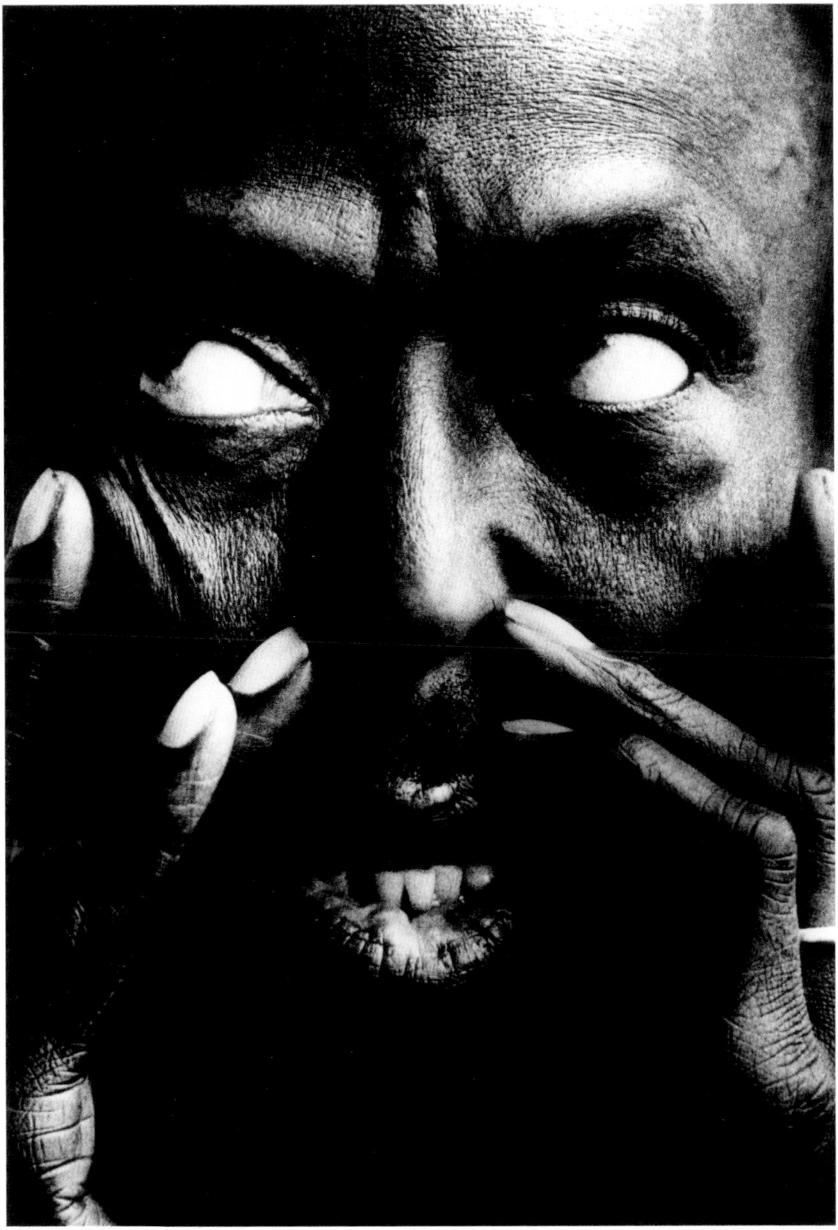

57 MILES DAVIS, MONTREAL, 1985

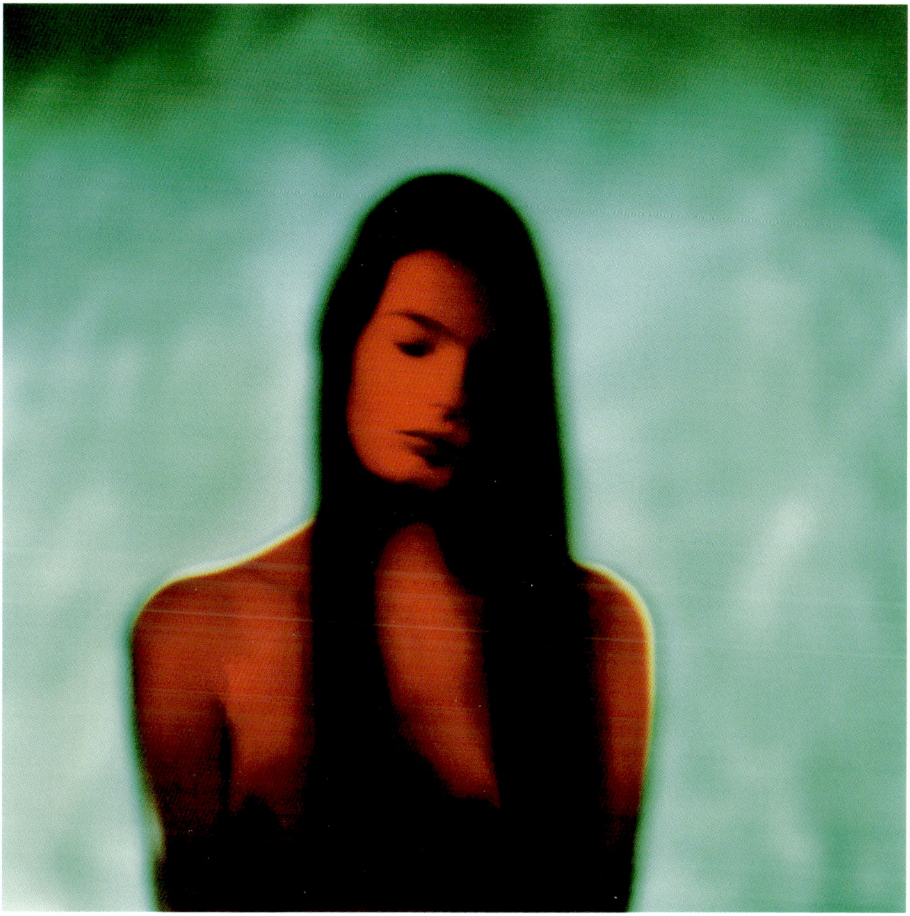

58 BARBARA III, LONDON, 1990

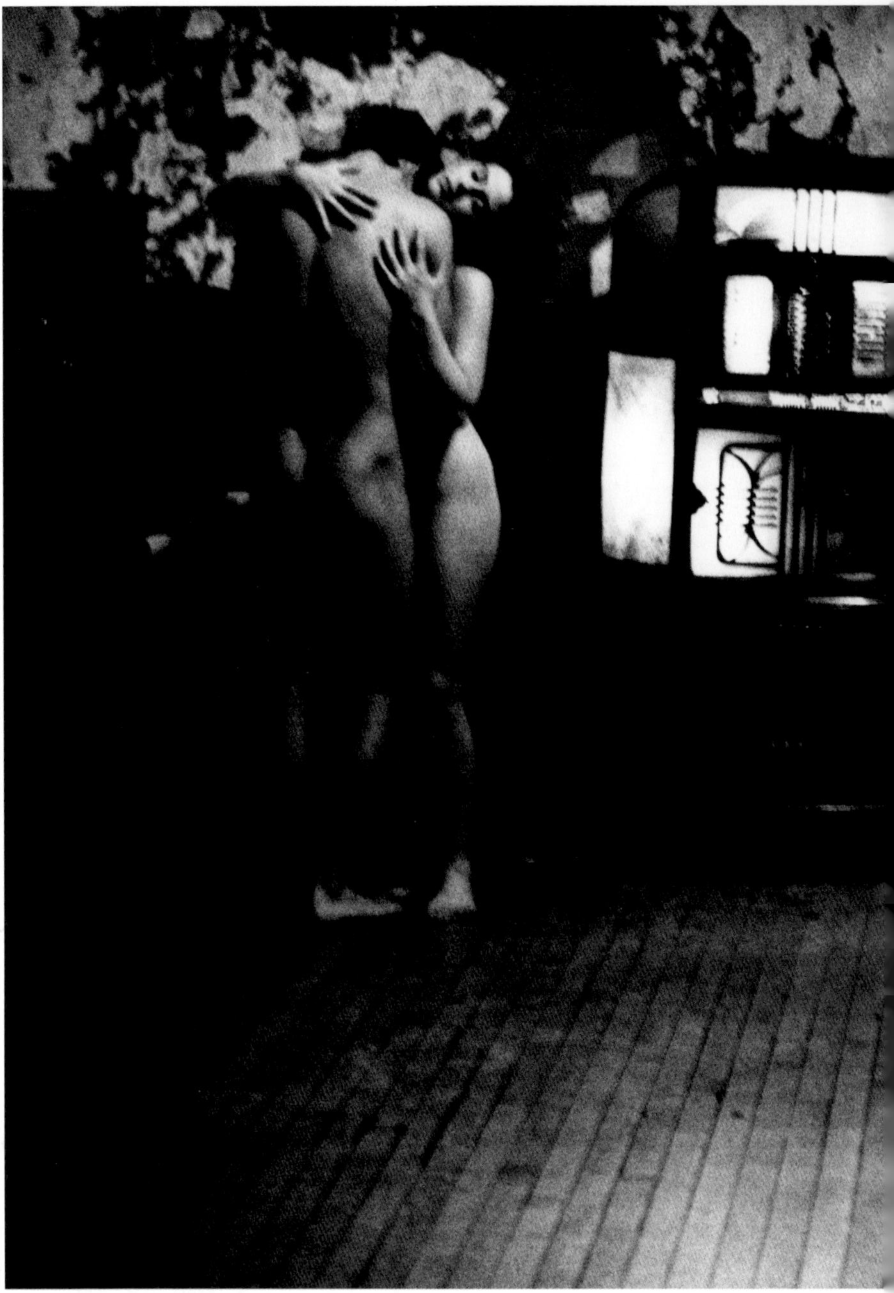

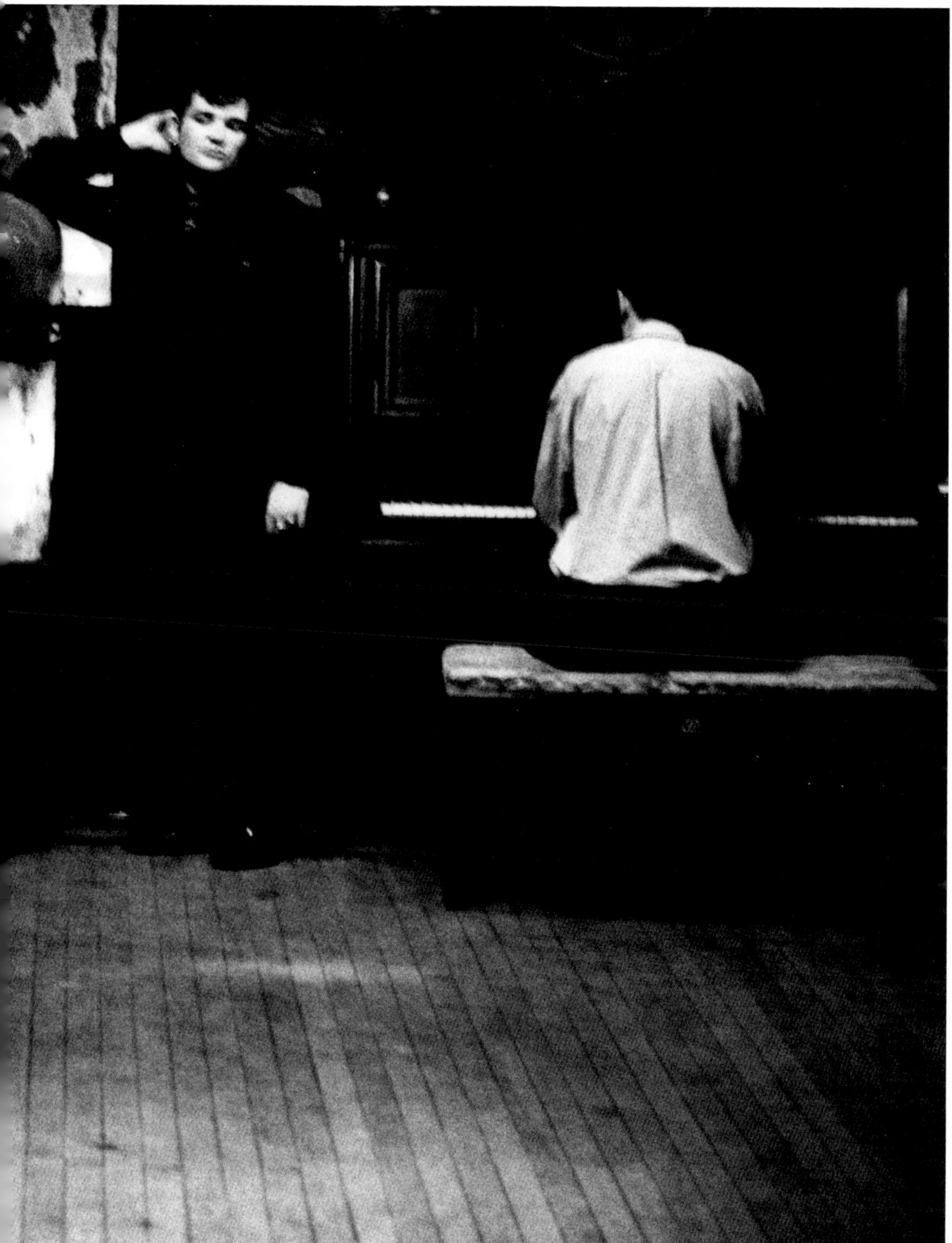

59 GAVIN FRIDAY, NEW YORK, 1988

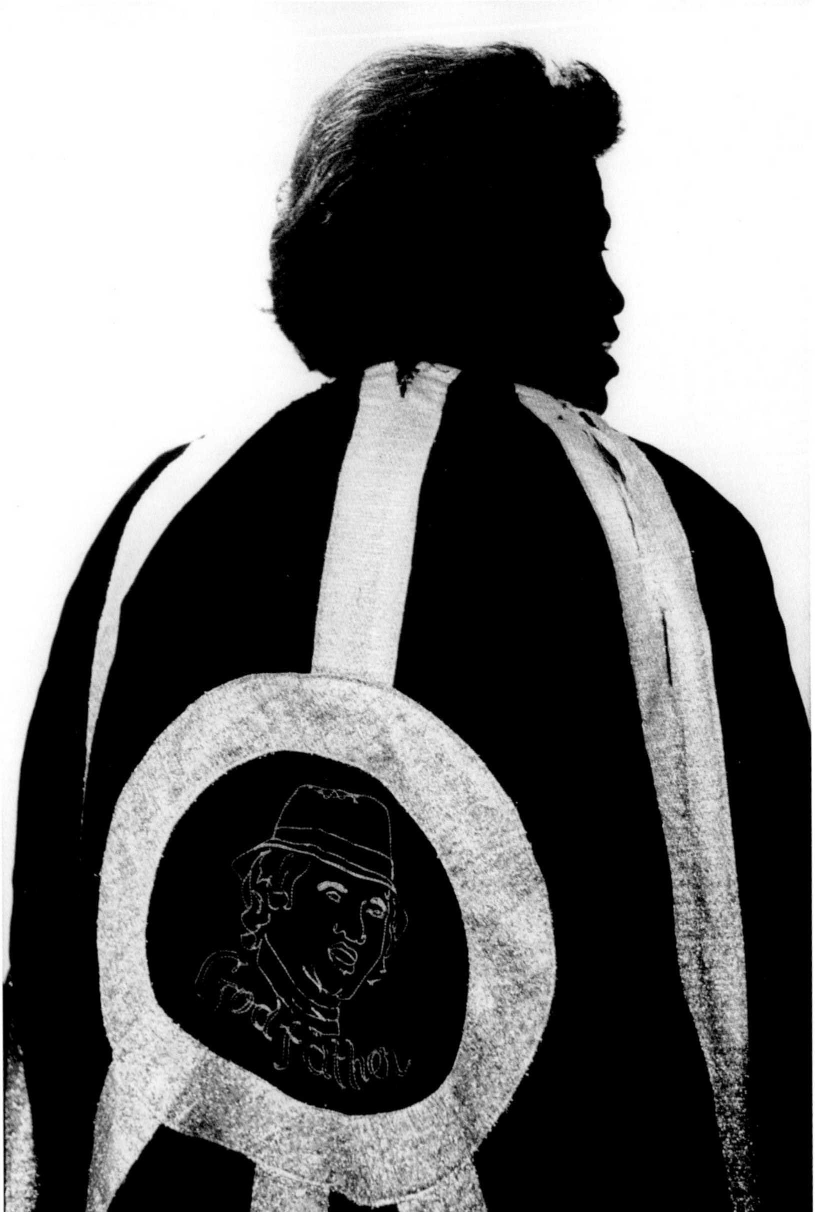

60 JAMES BROWN, LONDON, 1982

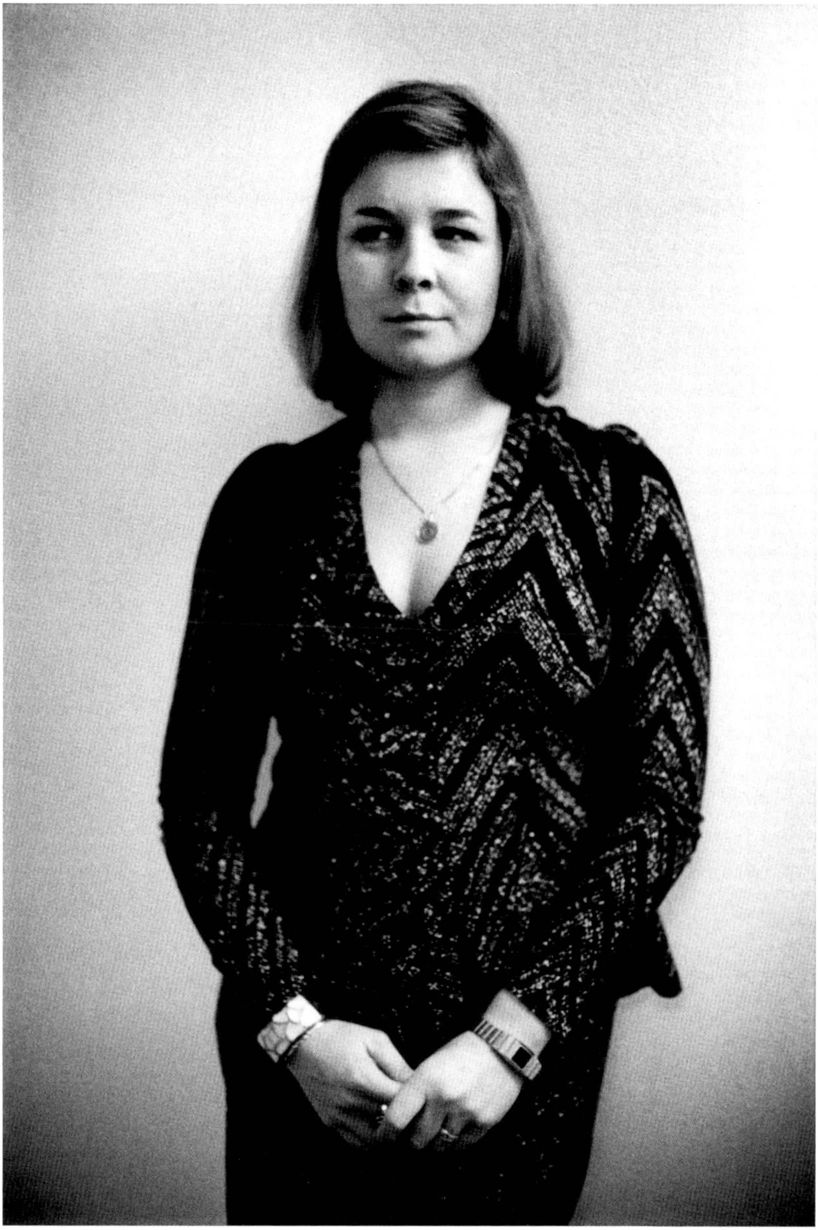

61 SANDY DENNY, GRONINGEN, 1975

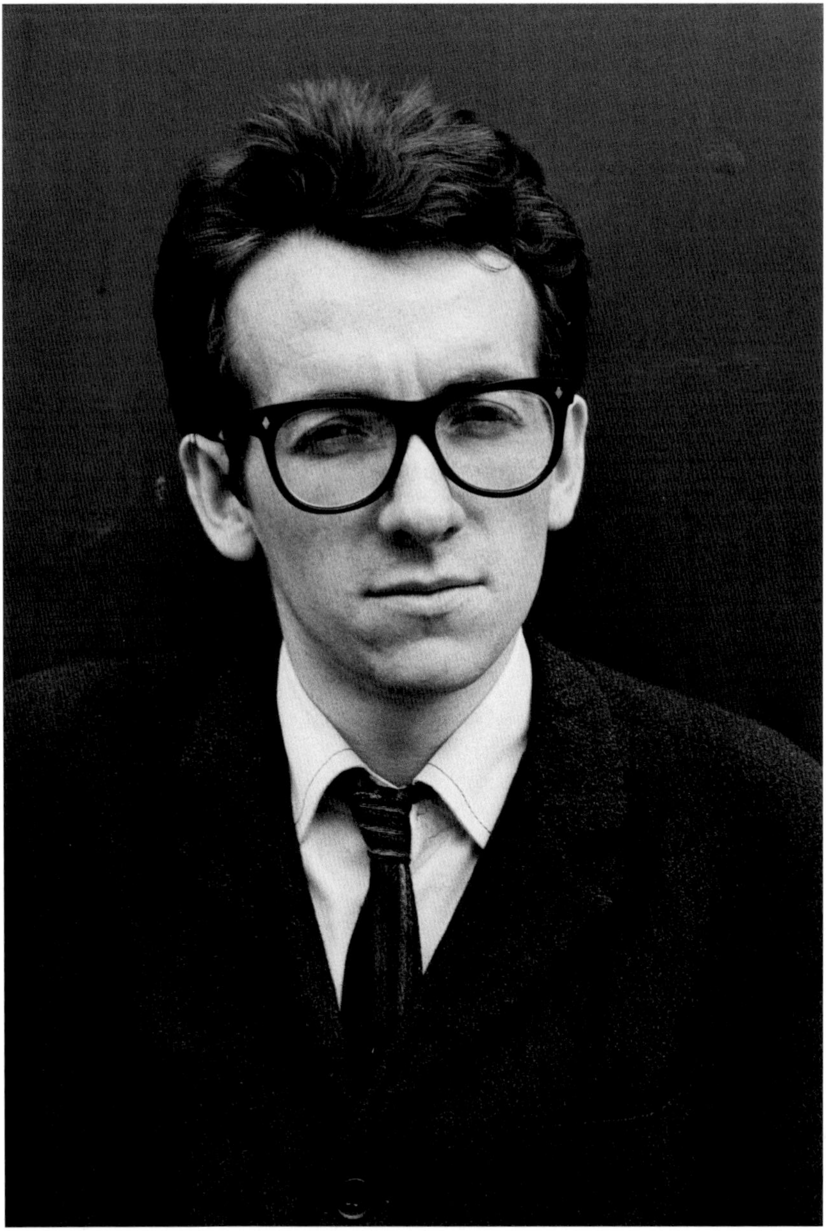

62 ELVIS COSTELLO, HILVERSUM, 1977

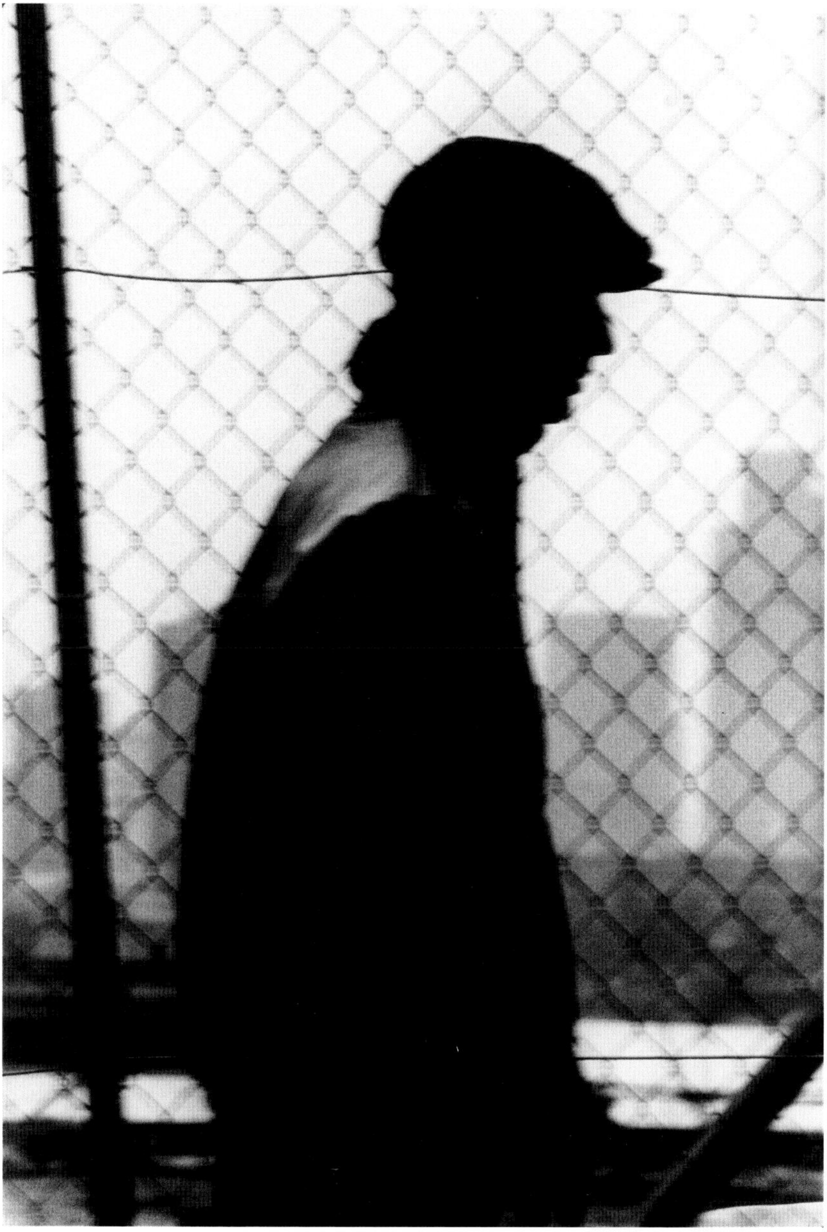

63 FRANK TOVEY, LONDON, 1988

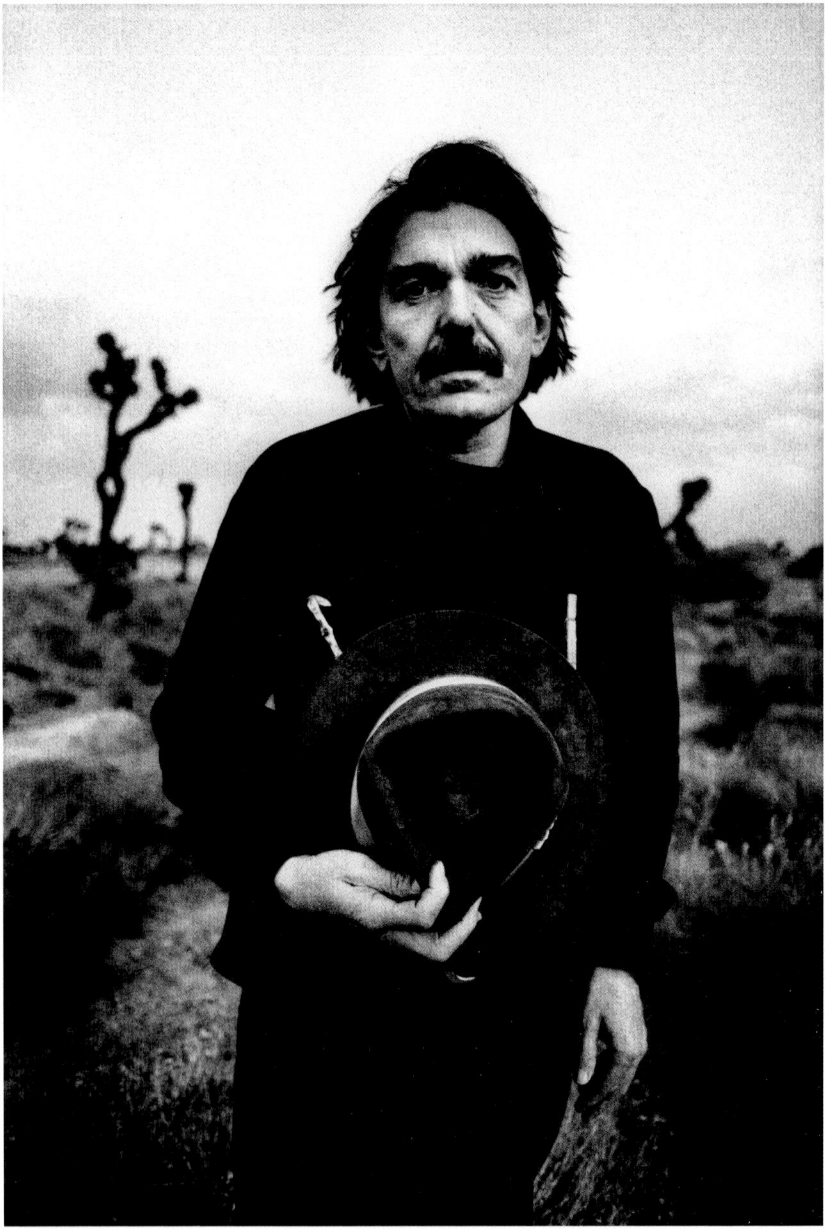

64 DON VAN VLIET, MOJAVE DESERT, 1980

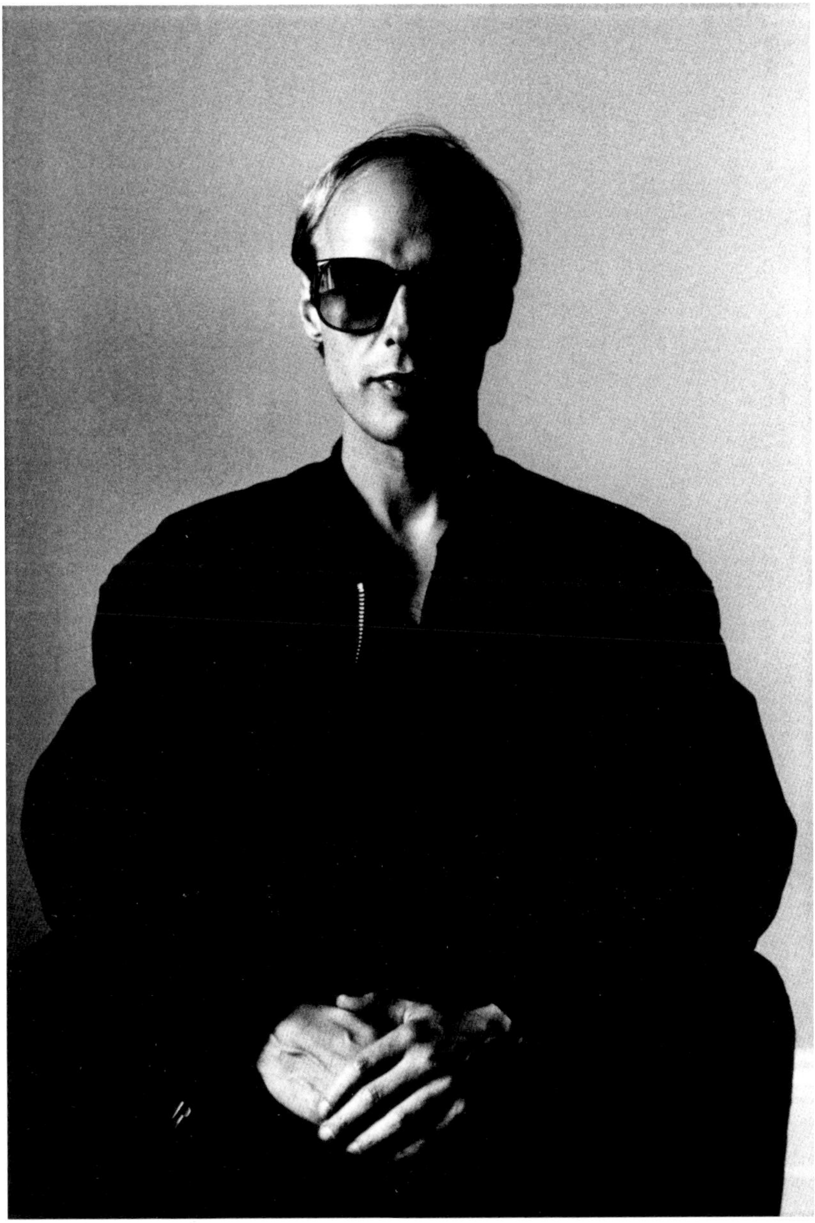

65 BRIAN ENO, LONDON, 1980

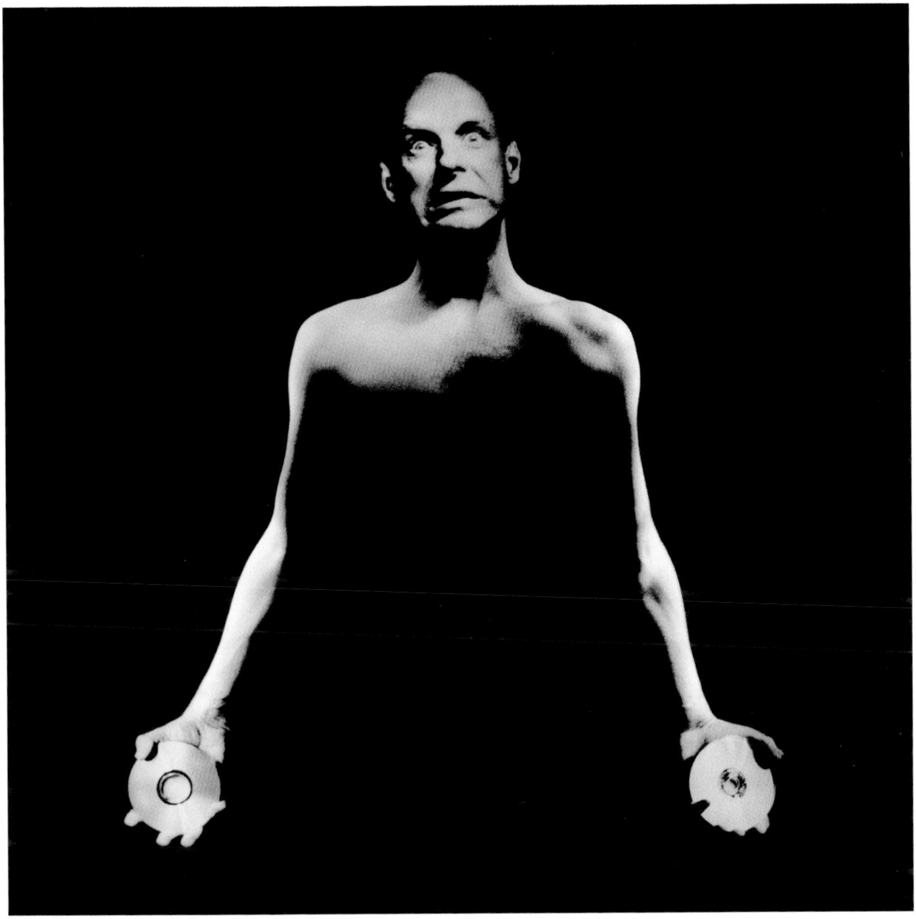

66 BRIAN ENO, LONDON, 1990

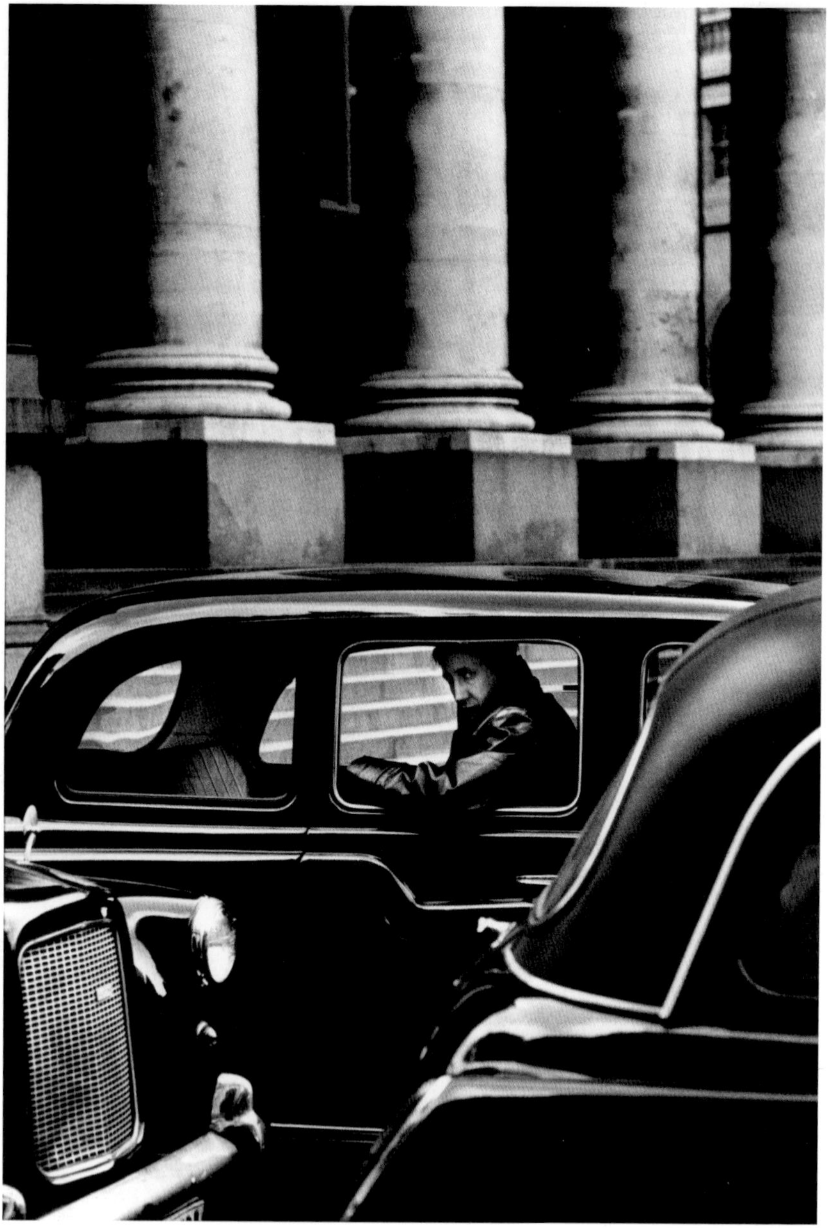

67 PETE TOWNSHEND, LONDON, 1982

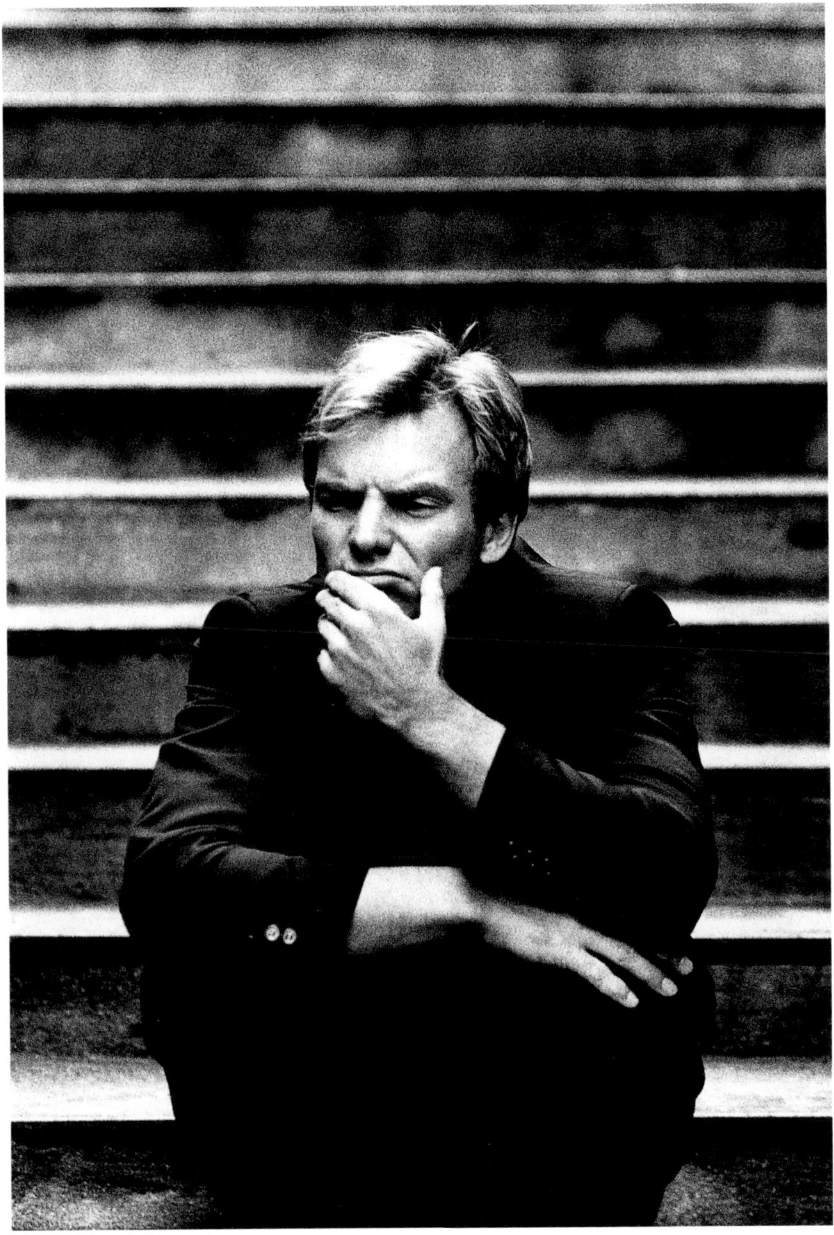

65 STING, PARIS, 1985

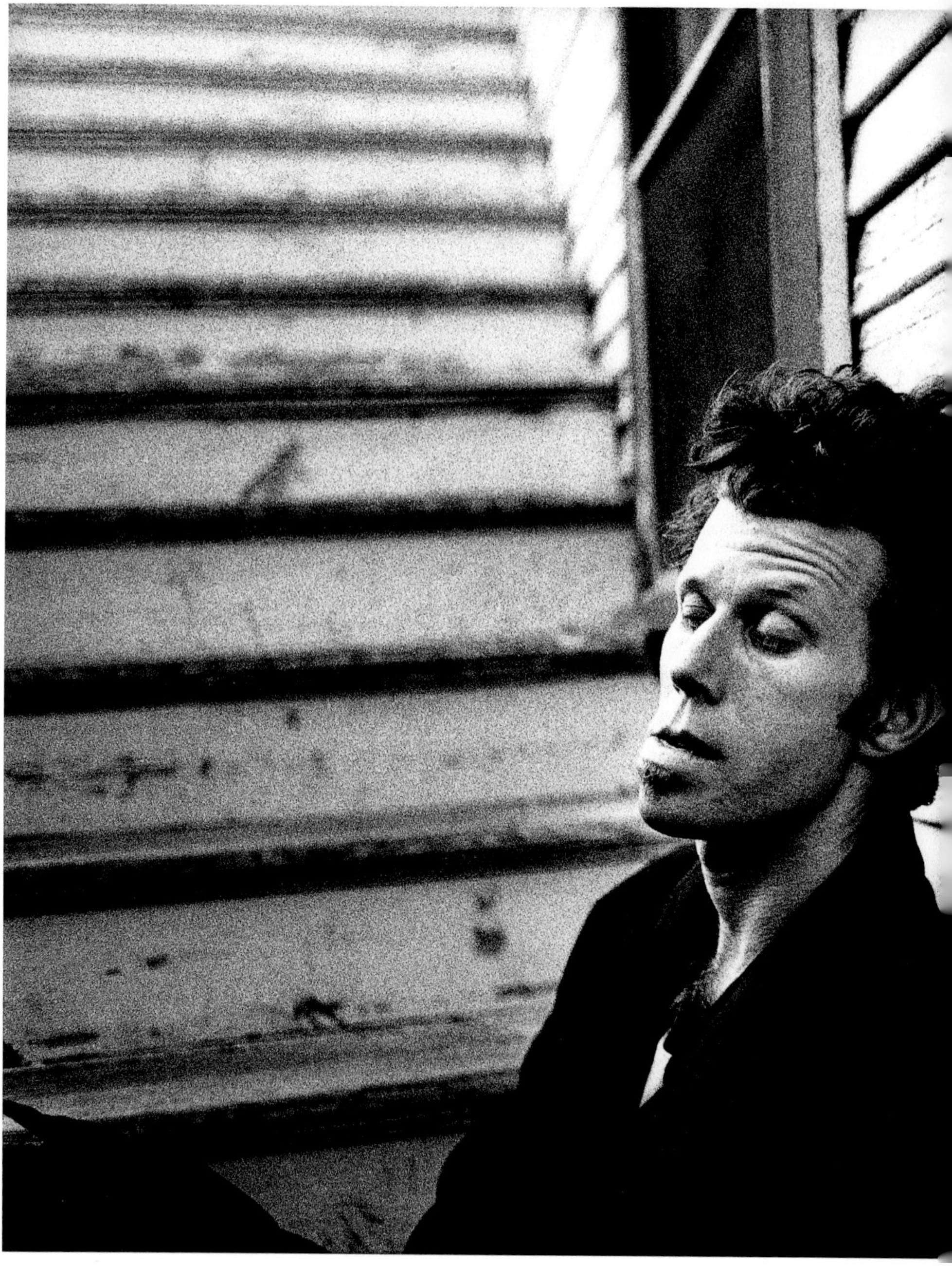

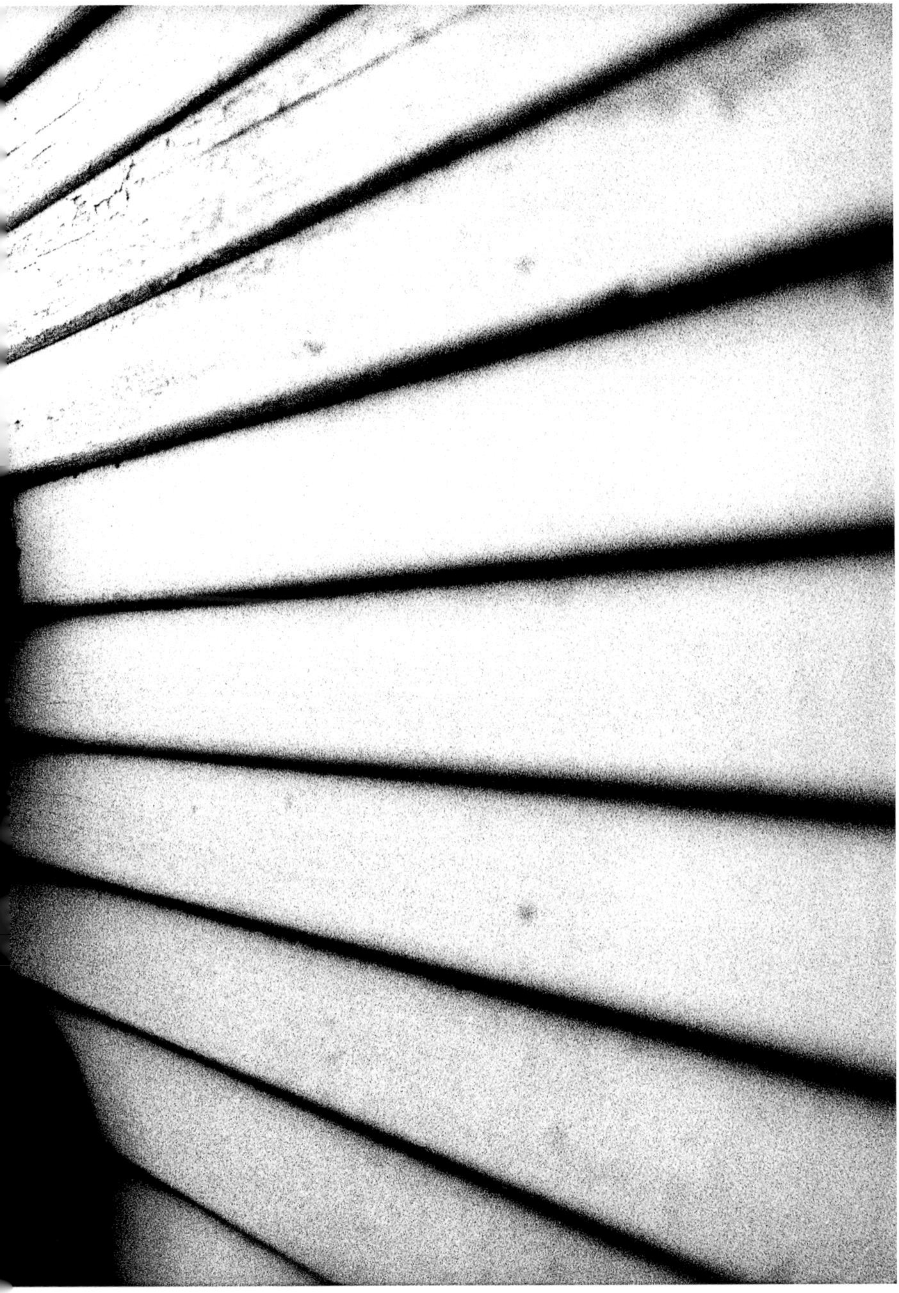

69 TOM WAITS, LOS ANGELES, 1983

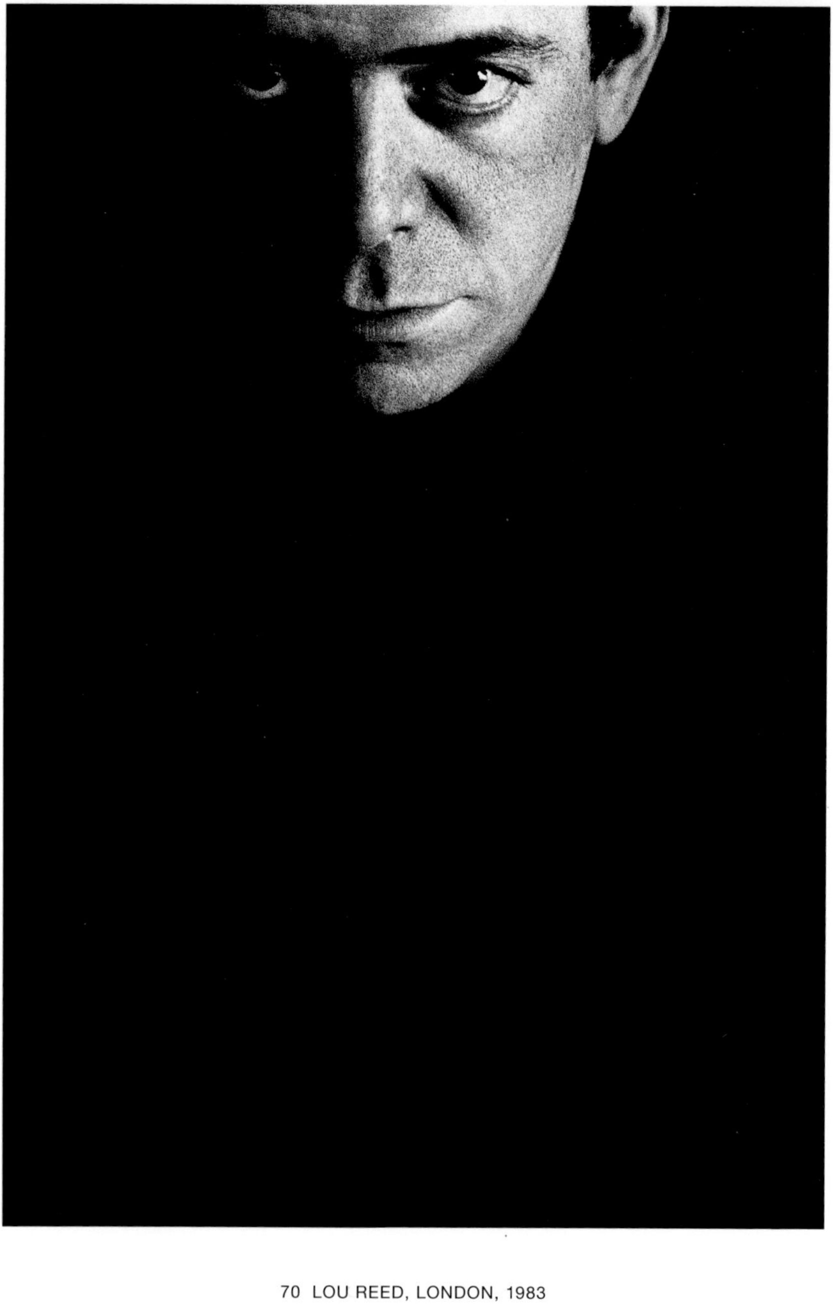

70 LOU REED, LONDON, 1983

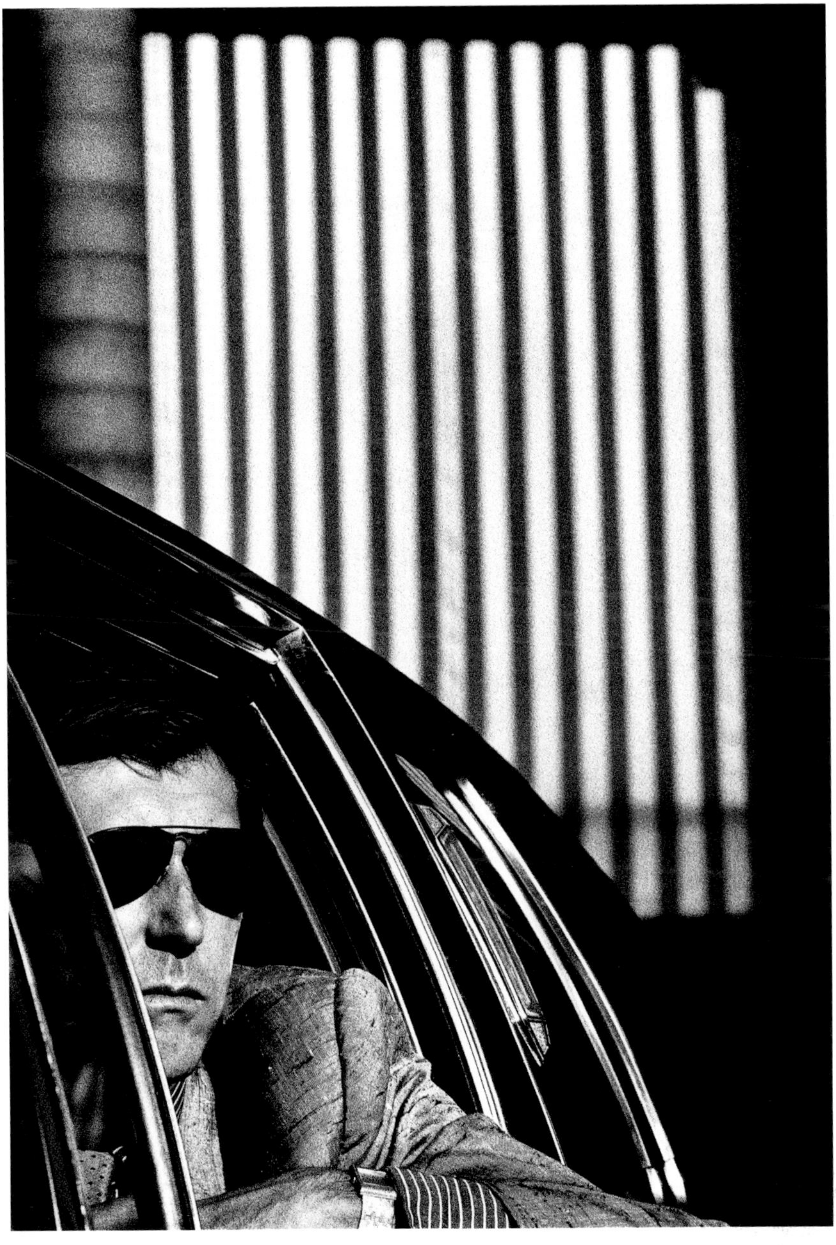

71 BRIAN FERRY, PARIS, 1982

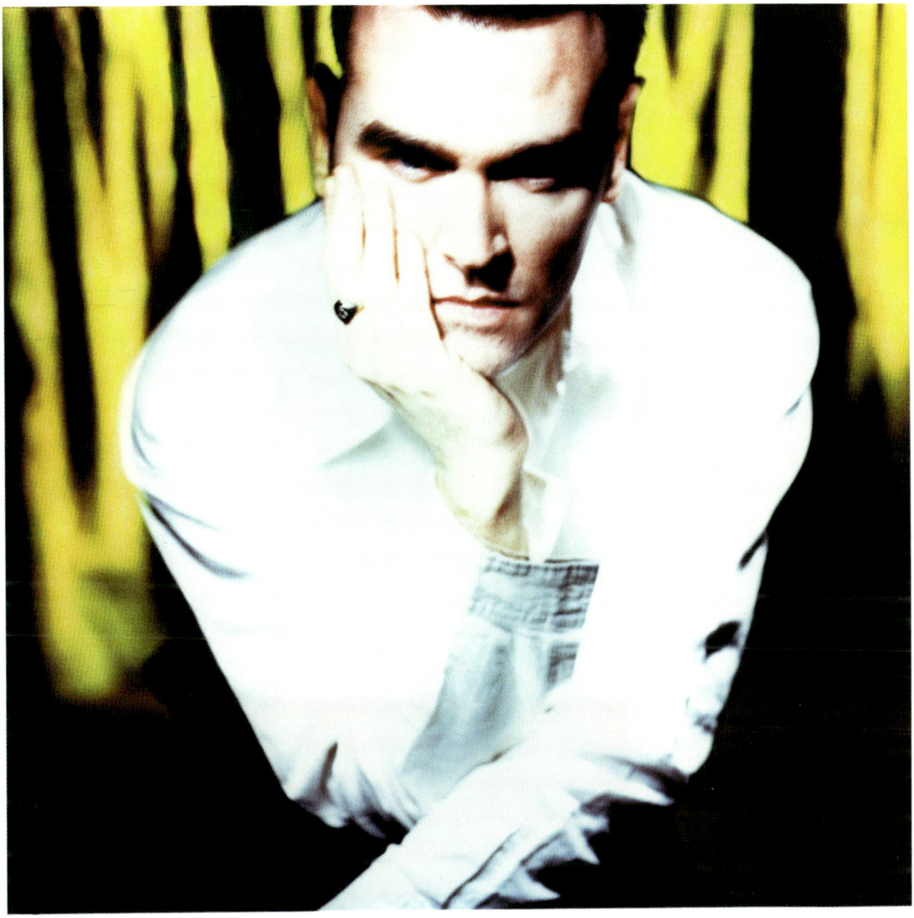

72 MORRISSEY, SUSSEX, 1989

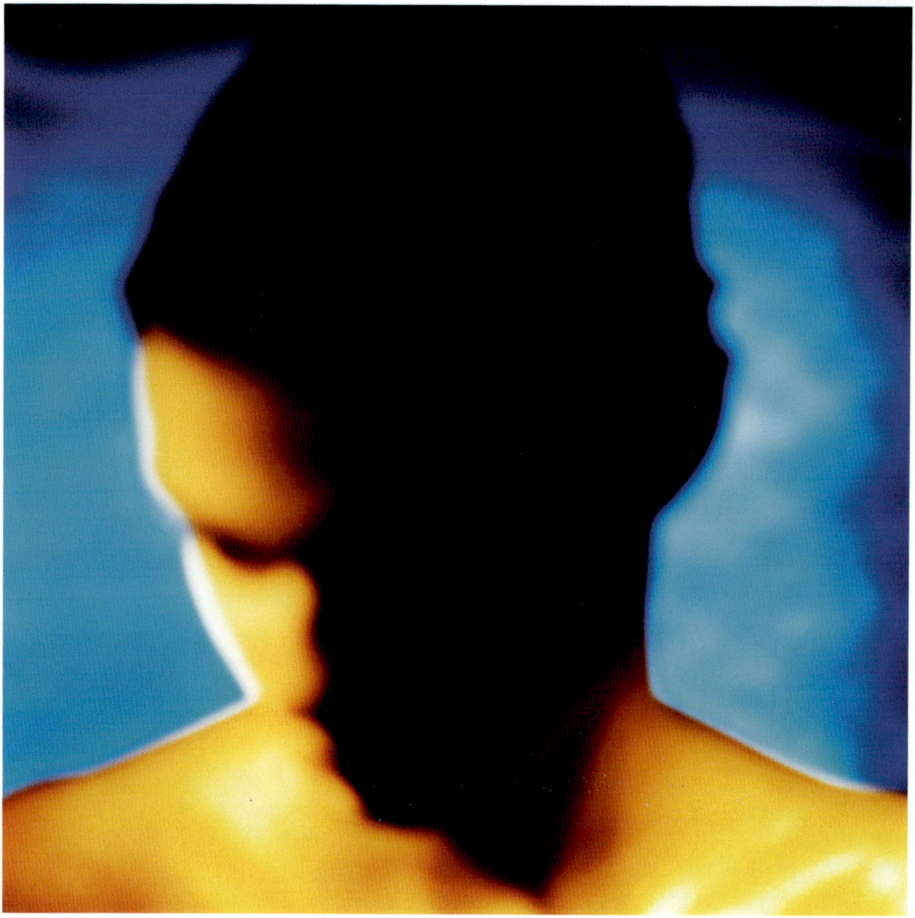

73 BARBARA I, LONDON, 1990

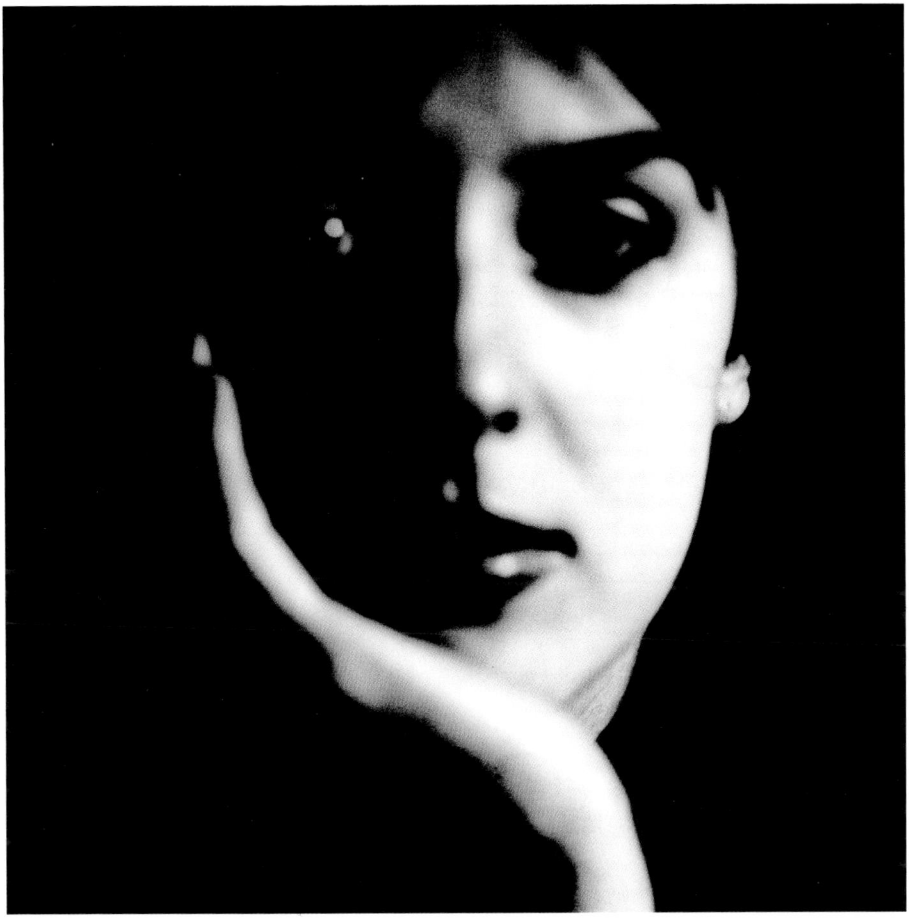

74 JULIE BURCHILL, LONDON, 1989

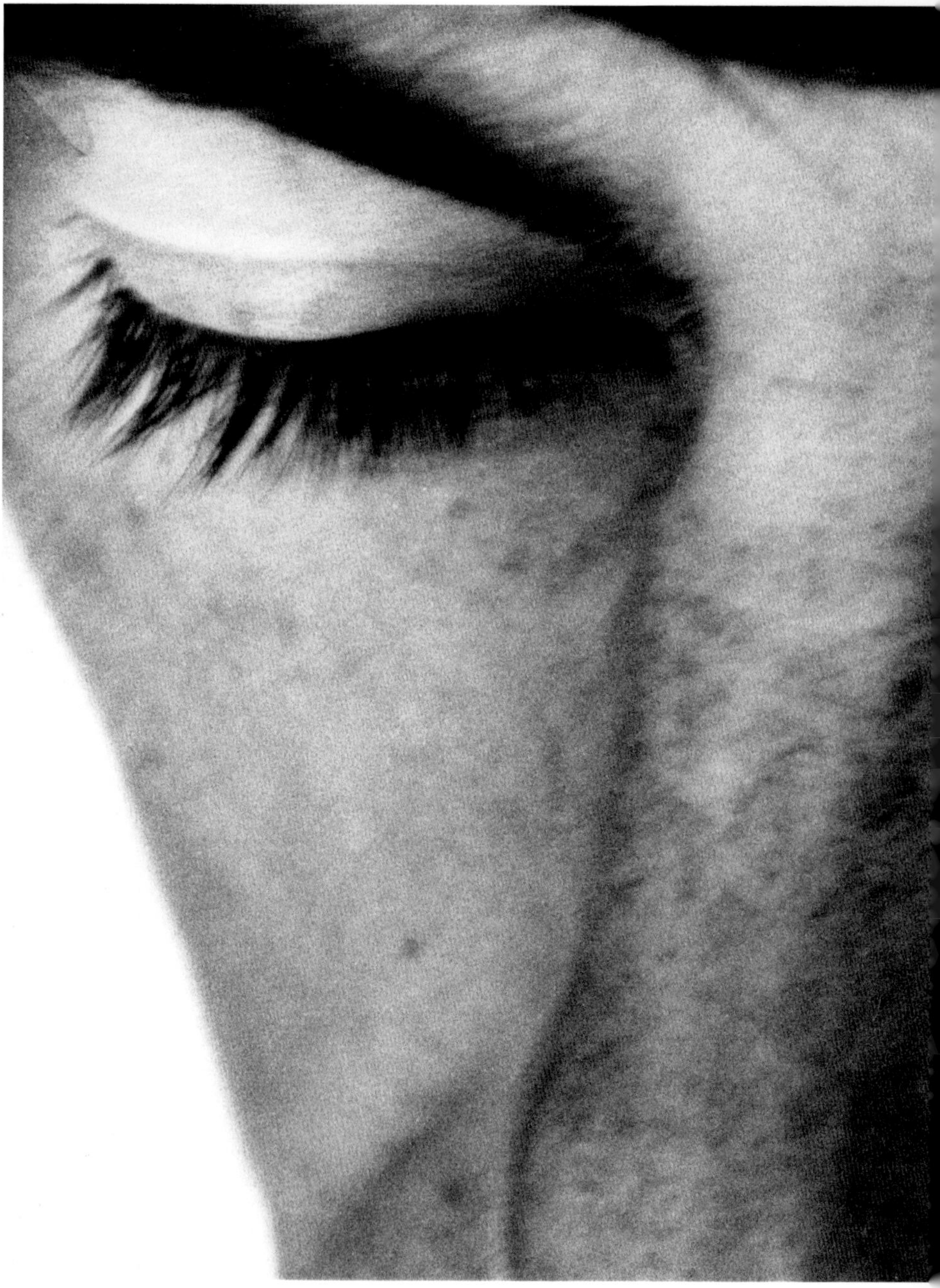

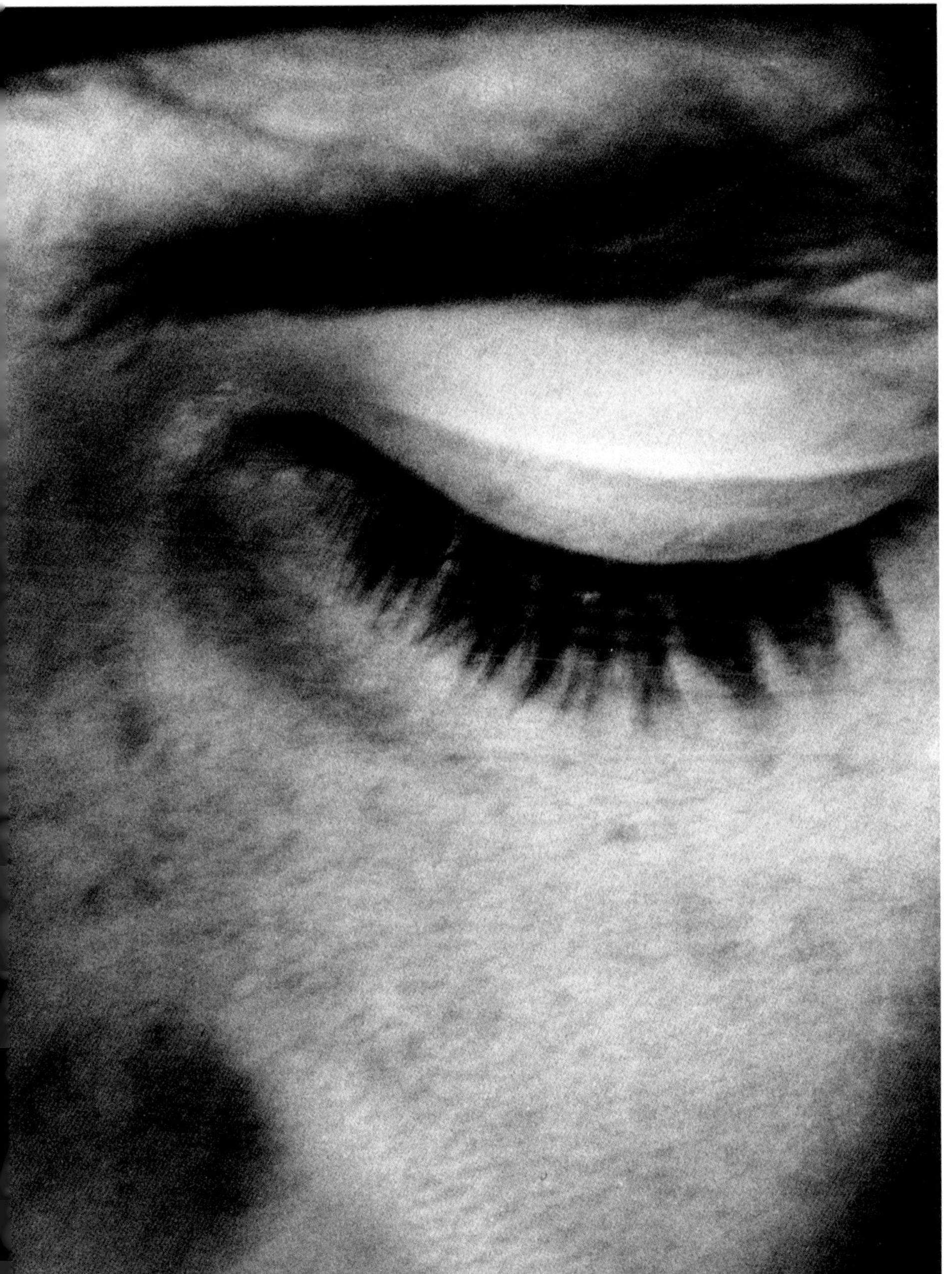

75 PETER HAMMILL, BATH, 1986

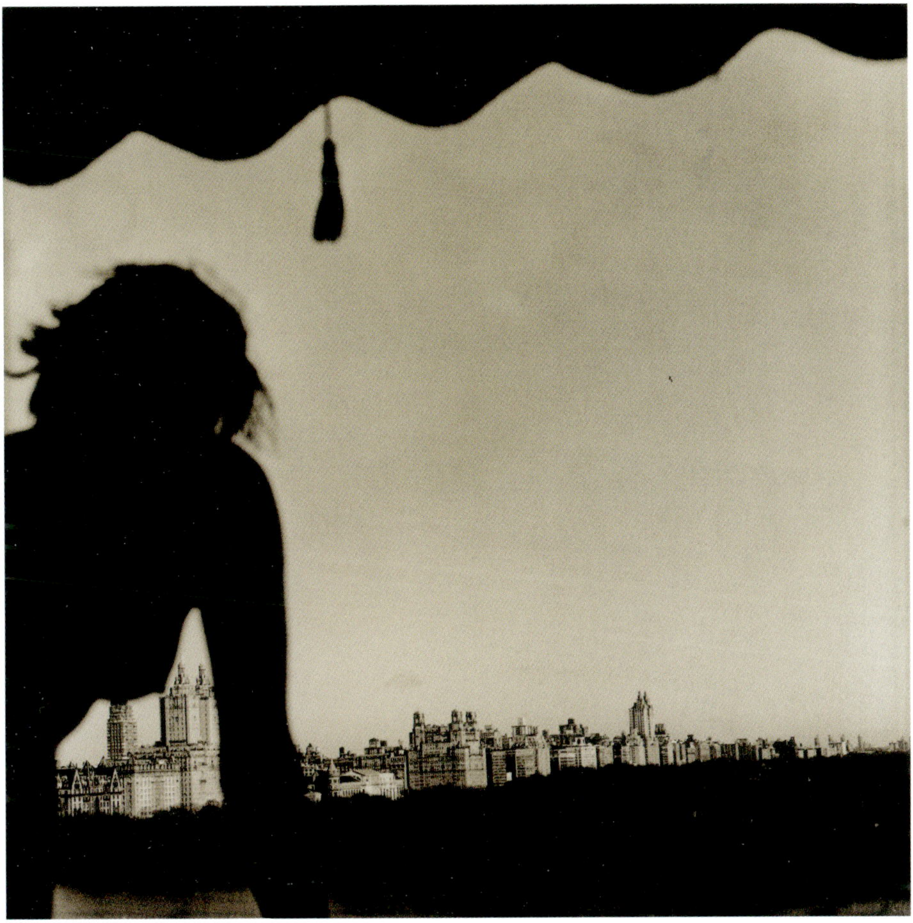

76 NASSIM, NEW YORK, 1988

ANTON CORBIJN

1955	born in Strijen, Netherlands
1972	first photographs taken at concert in Groningen, Netherlands, some get published
1973	meets Herman Brood whom he will photograph till Herman's death in 2001
1974	finishes High School and moves to The Hague
1976	sets off as a 'professional' photographer
1977	meets Johnny Rotten
	meets Tom Waits
1979	meets Siouxsie Sioux
	moves to London
	meets Joy Division
1980	becomes main photographer for the New Musical Express (NME)
	meets Captain Beefheart, David Bowie, The Slits, and countless other musicians
1981	meets Depeche Mode
1982	meets U2
1983	music video *Hockey* (Palais Schaumburg in Hamburg)
	meets Nick Cave
1985	meets Miles Davis
1988	meets Herbert Grönemeyer
1989	publication *Famouz*
1990	meets R.E.M.
1990/92	lives between Los Angeles and London
1993	designs stage for Depeche Mode's *Devotional* tour
	meets Nirvana
	short film *Some Yo Yo Stuff* on Don Van Vliet aka Captain Beefheart
1994	MTV Award for best 'alternative' video for Nirvana's *Heart Shaped Box*
1996	publication *Star Trak*
	meets Metallica
1999	publication *33 Still Lives*
	works with Marlene Dumas on strippinggirls series
2002	publication *a. somebody*
2005	publication *U2&i*
	dvd music videos *The Work of Director Anton Corbijn*
	CADS Award for Outstanding Achievement in the field of music videos
	meets Arcade Fire

2007	film *Control* premieres at Cannes Film Festival designs logo for city of The Hague Golden Frog in Lodz for contribution to music videos
2008	publication *In Control* which documents the making of the film *Control* moves back to the Netherlands U2 release *Linear*, Anton's film to go with the *No Line On The Horizon* record
2010	film *The American* and photo book *Inside the American* first show of *Inwards and Onwards*, New York
2011	exhibition and publication *Inwards and Onwards* FOAM, Amsterdam receives Prins Bernard Cultuurfonds Award
2013	publication *Waits/Corbijn* in collaboration with Tom Waits
2014	film *A Most Wanted Man* and photobook *Looking at A Most Wanted Man*
2015	film *LIFE* premieres at Berlinale, Berlin exhibition and publication *1-2-3-4* Fotomuseum, The Hague exhibition and publication *Hollands Deep* Gemeentemuseum, The Hague

SELECTED EXHIBITIONS

2015
Faces Now (groupshow) BoZaR, Bruxelles
1-2-3-4 Fotomuseum, The Hague
Hollands Deep Gemeentemuseum, The Hague

2014
New Squares Zeno X Gallery, Antwerp
a. somebody Leica at Photokina, Cologne
David Bowie is (group show) Martin-Gropius-Bau, Berlin

2013
Inwards and Onwards Kunstmuseum, Bochum
The Fashion World of Jean Paul Gaultier, 'From the Sidewalk to the Catwalk' (group show) The Brooklyn Museum, New York
David Bowie is (group show), Victoria & Albert Museum, London

2012
Inwards and Onwards Fotografiska Museet, Stockholm
R.E.M. Seen between 1990–2010 Staatliche Kunstsammlungen Dresden

2011
Inwards and Onwards Foam Museum, Amsterdam
American Dream (group show) DZ Bank Kunstsammlung, Frankfurt

2010
Inwards and Onwards Stellan Holm Gallery, New York
Inwards and Onwards Galerie Anita Beckers, Frankfurt

2009
Work (Munka) Ludwig Museum of Contemporary Art, Budapest
We Want Miles (group show) Musée de la Musique, Paris
Das Porträt. Fotografie als Bühne Kunstmuseum Vienna

2008
Retrospective Tennis Palace Art Museum, Helsinki
Retrospective Moscow Museum of Modern Art, Moscow

2006

Anton Corbijn Gallerie Lelong, Zurich
Herman Brood Groninger Museum, Groningen

2005

U2&i Stellan Holm Gallery, New York
U2&i C/O Berlin, Berlin
U2&i Torch Gallery, Amsterdam
Anton Corbijn Fotomuseum Provincie Antwerpen, Antwerp
22:U2 Michael Hoppen Gallery, London

2004

Anton Corbijn (Paul Huf/KLM Photography Award) Cobra Museum, Amstelveen
Anton Corbijn Palazzo Fortuny, Venice
The Drifter The Dreamer (group show) – Nederlands Fotomuseum, Rotterdam

2003

Mortalis (group show) GEM, The Hague
Anton Corbijn Galleria d'Arte Moderna, Bologna
Everybody Hurts Kestner Gesellschaft, Hannover
Zeno X Anniversary Show Zeno X Gallery, Antwerp

2002

Mortals Kulturhuset, Stockholm
Mortals Øksnehallen, Copenhagen
Anton Corbijn Leica Gallery, Prague
a. somebody Gemeentehuis Strijen, Strijen
a. somebody Galerie Anita Beckers, Frankfurt
a. somebody Richard Goodall Gallery, Manchester

2001

KPN Collectie (group show) Huis Marseille, Amsterdam
Anton Corbijn Photographs Govinda Gallery, Washington D.C.
WERK Münchner Stadtmuseum, Munich
WERK Museum Moderne Kunst, Dresden
Anton Corbijn Gemeentemuseum Helmond, Helmond

2000

Still Lives Torch Gallery, Amsterdam
WERK Groninger Museum, Groningen

Anton Corbijn Photographien Museum Bochum, Bochum
strippinggirls – with Marlene Dumas – S.M.A.K., Ghent

1999
Black, Brown and Blue David Beitzel Gallery, New York
Still Lives Galerie Anita Beckers, Frankfurt

1998
Recent Acquisitions DG Bank, Frankfurt
Dum umeni mesta Brna Haus der Kunst, Brno

1997
Corbijn Exponera/Foto Fair, Gothenburg
Anton Corbijn Photographs Fahey/Klein Gallery, Los Angeles
Anton Corbijn Castello di Rivoli, Turin
Fotoos Gemeentemuseum Helmond, Helmond

1996
Square Torch Gallery, Amsterdam
Anton Corbijn Zeno X Gallery, Antwerp
Star Trak Galerie Anita Beckers, Darmstadt
Anton Corbijn Fotografie Deichtorhallen, Hamburg

1994
Innit? Kunsthal, Rotterdam
Anton Corbijn Stedelijk Museum, Amsterdam

1993
Hugo Erfurth Preis Museum Morsbroich, Leverkusen

1991
Groninger Museum Collection Institut Neerlandais, Paris

1990
Anton Corbijn City Centre Gallery, Dublin

1989
Famouz Torch Gallery, Amsterdam
Famouz Parco Gallery, Tokyo
Famouz Parco Gallery, Kyoto